Studies in Caribbean Languages

Chief Editor: John R. Rickford
Managing Editor: Joseph T. Farquharson

In this series:

1. Irvine-Sobers, G. Alison. The acrolect in Jamaica: The architecture of phonological variation.

2. Forbes-Barnett, Marsha. Dual aspectual forms and event structure in Caribbean English Creoles.

3. Sherriah, André Ché. A tale of two dialect regions: Sranan's 17th-century English input.

Dual aspectual forms and event structure in Caribbean English Creoles

Marsha Forbes-Barnett

Marsha Forbes-Barnett. 2019. *Dual aspectual forms and event structure in Caribbean English Creoles* (Studies in Caribbean Languages 2). Berlin: Language Science Press.

This title can be downloaded at:
http://langsci-press.org/catalog/book/80
© 2019, Marsha Forbes-Barnett
Published under the Creative Commons Attribution 4.0 Licence (CC BY 4.0):
http://creativecommons.org/licenses/by/4.0/
ISBN: 978-3-96110-112-2 (Digital)
　　　978-3-96110-113-9 (Hardcover)

DOI:10.5281/zenodo.1476426
Source code available from www.github.com/langsci/80
Collaborative reading: paperhive.org/documents/remote?type=langsci&id=80

Cover and concept of design: Ulrike Harbort
Typesetting: Felix Kopecky, Sebastian Nordhoff
Proofreading: Andreas Hölzl, Eitan Grossman, Jean Nitzke, Jeffrey Pheiff, Jeroen van de Weijer, Linda Leembruggen, Melanie Röthlisberger, Paulson Skerrit, Prisca Jerono & Vadim Kimmelman
Fonts: Linux Libertine, Libertinus Math, Arimo, DejaVu Sans Mono
Typesetting software: XƎLATEX

Language Science Press
Unter den Linden 6
10099 Berlin, Germany
langsci-press.org

Storage and cataloguing done by FU Berlin

Contents

Abbreviations   v

1 **Introduction**   1
    1.1   Background   1
    1.2   Outer/viewpoint Aspect   1
    1.3   Compositionality   3
         1.3.1   Viewpoint aspect and inherent aspect   3
         1.3.2   Progressive aspect and stativity   4
    1.4   Inner Aspect   5
    1.5   Aspect in CECs and the nature of the verb   6
    1.6   A note on the compositionality of Aspect   8
    1.7   Dual aspect and the Stative/Non-stative distinction   9
    1.8   The proposal   11
    1.9   Aim and scope of this work   12
    1.10   The organisation of the work   15

2 **Aspect in Caribbean English Creoles: An overview of works**   19
    2.1   Background   19
    2.2   Some contributions to the study of Aspect in CECs   20
         2.2.1   Voorhoeve (1957)   20
         2.2.2   Alleyne (1980)   24
         2.2.3   Bickerton (1975)   28
         2.2.4   Bickerton (1981/2016)   33
         2.2.5   Jaganauth (1987)   34
         2.2.6   Winford (1993)   40
         2.2.7   Andersen (1990)   43
         2.2.8   Sidnell (2002)   45
         2.2.9   Gooden (2008)   48
         2.2.10   Youssef (2003)   51
    2.3   Observations   54

Contents

3	**The problem of dual aspectual forms**	**57**
3.1	Introduction	57
3.2	Verb or adjective? The categorial status of property items	58
	3.2.1 The Sranan case: A debate between Sebba and Seuren	58
	3.2.2 Kouwenberg (1996)	65
	3.2.3 A note on later works	67
3.3	The question of the Stative/Non-stative distinction	68
3.4	Winford's semantic categorisation of CEC property items and an evaluation	71
	3.4.1 Winford's semantic categorisation of CEC property items	71
	3.4.2 An evaluation	73
3.5	Summary of observations	82

4	**The Stative/Non-stative distinction and change as a lexico-semantic concept**	**85**
4.1	Introduction	85
4.2	The stative/non-stative distinction and the notion of Change	87
4.3	Event structures and primitives of change	90
	4.3.1 Event types and structures	91
	4.3.2 State	91
	4.3.3 Transition	93
	4.3.4 Process	93
4.4	Primitives of Change	96
	4.4.1 BECOME and CAUSE	97
	4.4.2 DO	100
4.5	More on Change: Transitivity alternations	101
	4.5.1 CAUSE and BECOME in the middle and causative/inchoative alternations	102
	4.5.2 CONTACT in the body-part possessor ascension alternation	103
	4.5.3 MOTION + CONTACT in the conative alternation	104
4.6	Observations	105

5	**Syntactic behaviour, event types and semantic interpretations**	**107**
5.1	Background	107
5.2	Criteria for the categorisation of property items	109
	5.2.1 Non-stative use: The progressive criterion	109
	5.2.2 Non-stative use: Transitive alternation	112
	5.2.3 Event types and semantic interpretations: State, Transition and Process	113

	5.3	Property items in JC: Towards a classification	116
		5.3.1 Transitions in JC	116
		5.3.2 States among JC property items	121
		5.3.3 On the Non-stative use of State items	124
	5.4	A classification of property items in JC	129
	5.5	Summary	131
6	Summing up: On the categorial status of dual aspectual forms		133
	6.1	Overview	133
	6.2	On the categorial status of dual aspectual forms	135
		6.2.1 Class 1 property items as Non-stative verbs	136
		6.2.2 Class 2 property items as (Stative) adjectives	140
	6.3	Contribution to scholarship	143
	6.4	Scope for further study	146

References   149

Index   155

   Name index   155

   Language index   157

   Subject index   159

Abbreviations

BC	Belizean Creole
CEC	Caribbean English Creole
ES	Event structure
GC	Guyanese Creole
GU	Gullah
JC	Jamaican Creole
MOC	Measuring Out Constraint
SM	Saramaccan
SR	Sranan
SPD	State–Process distinction
TMA	Tense Mood Aspect

1 Introduction

1.1 Background

Comrie's (1976) definition of Aspect[1] as "the internal temporal constituency of a situation" (p. 3) does not begin to capture the complex nature of Aspect as articulated in the literature. Indeed, "the internal constituency of a situation" is elaborated as a mix of information from the verb, internal and external arguments, grammatical aspect markers, adverbials etc. (cf. Klein 1994; Krifka 1998; Jackendoff 1996; MacDonald 2008; Mourelatos 1981; Ramchand 2008; Rothstein 2004; Tenny 1994; Tenny & Pustejovsky 2000; Verkuyl 1996; 1999) among others. The involvement of these elements effectively establishes Aspect as two domains of study, namely inner and outer aspect (Travis 1991; 2005; Verkuyl 1996), or situation and viewpoint aspect (Smith 1983; 1991).

In the sections which follow I will look briefly at viewpoint aspect (§1.2) and inner aspect (§1.3). Further to this, I will look with specific regard at the case for further investigations into the nature of the verb itself in the study of Aspect in Caribbean English Creoles (CECs) (Section §1.4). In §1.5 I will look at the compositionality of Aspect and move into a discussion of dual aspect and the Stative/Non-stative distinction in §1.6. In §1.7 I present a synopsis of my proposal in this study. The aim and scope of the work is presented in §1.8 while the organisation of the work is presented in §1.9.

1.2 Outer/viewpoint Aspect

Outer aspect or viewpoint aspect may be taken to refer to the impact of grammatical aspect markers in the construct of aspectual outlook. The most well-known distinction in this area is that established in the Perfective and Imperfective (see Comrie 1976). According to Comrie (1976), the Perfective is "the view of a situation as a single whole, without distinction of the separate phases that make up

---

[1] I will use the term "Aspect" in this work in reference to the general concept as opposed to specific levels that are involved. I will use the lower case "aspect" to refer to specific levels or elements of Aspect such as grammatical aspect, or inner and outer aspect.

1 Introduction

that situation." (p. 16). By contrast, the Imperfective "pays essential attention to the internal structure of the situation." (p. 16).

Languages have various ways of dealing with the expression of these aspectual viewpoints which may or may not be grammaticalized in languages. Thus for example, while the English language employs the use of the progressive *-ing* to express Imperfectivity, a language such as Finnish uses case marking to establish the difference between a Perfective and Imperfective viewpoint. Cf. (1)

(1) Finnish (Comrie 1976: 8)
    a. hän luki kirjan
       'He read the book.'
    b. hän luki kirjaa
       'He was reading the book.'

According to Travis (2010) discussion of the Finnish examples in (1), it is the partitive case in (1b) that results in the Imperfective reading as opposed to the accusative case in (1a) where we get a Perfective viewpoint (p. 2). Case does not play a similar role in English which, instead, employs the Progressive marking to focus on the internal aspect of the situation in the translation in (1b) whereas, the Perfective viewpoint is grammatically unmarked.

Semantically, viewpoint aspect has been indicated to be subjective in that a speaker may choose to express a particular perspective of a situation regardless of the inherent truth properties of the situation itself. Thus as Guéron (2008) points out, expressions of viewpoint aspect are "unaffected by real world experience" (p. 1824). Based on this, in the case of the examples in (1) above; both (1a) and (1b) may be true at the same time dependent on "the speaker's choice of perspective on the situation" (Smith 1983: 479).

In my discussion of the literature on Aspect in Caribbean English Creoles (CECs) in Chapter 2, we will see that Imperfective aspect in CECs is typically marked preverbally by a particle which has been analysed as marking Progressive, Imperfective, continuative or iterative depending on the author. Perfective, on the other hand is unmarked in CECs. It will become evident in Chapter 2 that the interaction between the notion of Stativity and Imperfective aspect marking is one that underpins the controversy that has existed in the field as it relates to the question of Stativity. My elaboration of this in Chapter 4 is intended to bring a measure of balance to this discussion.

1.3 Compositionality

1.3.1 Viewpoint aspect and inherent aspect

Viewpoint aspect has been indicated to interact with inherent aspect resulting either in a modification of the viewpoint typically associated with a marker or in a modification of the situation aspect inherently associated with the verb. Thus, in the case of the Progressive *-ing* morpheme in English we observe differences in interpretations as it interacts with different types of verbs, the typically Stative verb *have* (2) as well as with the Non-statives *run* and *close* in (3) and (4):

(2) (adapted from Lyons 1977: 707)
   a. She **has** a headache. (Stative)
   b. She **is having** a headache. (Non-stative)
   c. She **is having** one of her headaches. (Non-stative)

(3) John **is running**. (Non-stative)

(4) a. The door is **closed**. (Stative)
   b. The door **is closing**. (Non-stative)

Upon superficial examination, the Progressive viewpoint aspect associated with the *-ing* morpheme appears simply to establish a processual viewpoint. Upon closer examination however, it is noteworthy that the Stative interpretation typically associated with a verb like *have* in (2) shifts to one that is Non-stative analogous to that which is inherently associated with verbs like *run* and *close* as shown in (3) and (4). This is not the only noteworthy point however as further to this, one may analyse differences in the aspectual viewpoints that arise in each case. In particular, I note that, the use of the Progressive in the case of *have a headache* as in (2b–c) extends the situation, establishing the situation as on-going (cf. Guéron 2008). This is similar to the interpretation that we get in the case of *run* in (3) – both may be taken as having occurred and on-going in this context. In other words *John is running* must be taken to encompass the meanings: John HAS RUN as well as John CONTINUES to RUN. Similarly, She is HAVING a headache implies that She CONTINUES to have a headache that arose prior to the time of the utterance. The same is not true of the verb *close* in (4b) as *the door is closing* does not entail that the door has closed. Rather, (4b) must be interpreted as a Change of state in progress.

This difference in interpretations that arises where Progressive viewpoint aspect interacts with different types of verbs, I analyse as directly linked to the Event Structure (ES) that is inherently associated with particular verbs. While

1 Introduction

generally speaking the presence of Progressive viewpoint aspect signals the presence of Non-stative meaning, the nuances associated with this interaction are far more interesting and significant than the actual presence of Non-stative meaning. Thus, as we can see here, while the Progressive *-ing* morpheme in the case of an inherently Stative verb like *have* is responsible for the introduction of Non-stative meaning, this meaning is already present in the case of a verb like *run* where the Progressive simply establishes the situation as on-going. In the case of a verb like *close* which I analyse as a Change of state predicate (cf. Pustejovsky 1988) the viewpoint established on the situation is one which focuses on the onset of the situation within the context of a Change of state in progress. I return to examples such as these in §5.2 of this work.

Below I will look briefly look within the compositionality of aspect at the restriction on the combination of Progressive aspect and Stativity that has been cited in the literature.

1.3.2 Progressive aspect and stativity

A restriction has also been noted between Stative predicates, and Progressive viewpoint aspect (see Vendler 1957, Dowty 1979, Smith 1983 etc). Regarding this, Smith (1983) for example notes in relation to the examples in (5) below that the "same choices [in aspectual viewpoint] may not be available for talking about every situation" (p. 479).

(5) (Smith 1983: 479)
    a. You know the answer.
    b. * You are knowing the answer.

The ungrammaticality resulting from the interaction between a stative predicate such as *know* and the progressive *-ing* in the case of English has presented a case for many on the restriction between stativity and progressivity. However, as Smith (1983) points out "things are a little more complicated than this. Speakers sometimes make an unusual choice of aspect; i.e., one can talk about a situation in a manner not usually associated with it" (p. 479). Essentially, there may be occasions where a speaker may quite appropriately say "I am now knowing that!"

In dealing with this interaction between viewpoint aspect and other areas of Aspect, Smith (1983) in her speaker-based approach, cautions that "the properties of an actual situation should not be confused with its presentation in a given sentence" (p. 480) supporting the observation in the previous section. In Chapter 5 (§5.2) I attempt to treat this issue further where I explain my interpretation of the progressive criterion and its application in the model I articulate. More generally, while this area of Aspect will not constitute a major focus in this work, it will be highlighted in Chapter 2 as a principal area of focus in the study of Aspect in CECs.

Below I will look briefly at the area of inner aspect.

1.4 Inner Aspect

The domain of inner aspect refers to the interaction between the verb and its internal argument and concerns the aspectual feature associated with whether or not a situation has a "distinct, definite and inherent endpoint in time" (Tenny 1994: 4). Inner aspect has been of major interest in recent investigations into the syntax-semantics interface and has been characterised by several distinctions concerned with the notion of Endpoint. These include the Telic/Atelic Garey 1957; Comrie 1976; Smith 1991; Rothstein 2004, the Bounded/Non-bounded (Verkuyl 1972; Dahl 1981; 1985; Jackendoff 1990; Krifka 1998), the Culminating/Non-culminating (Moens & Steedman 1988), Delimited/Non-delimited (Mourelatos 1981; Tenny 1994) and Quantized/Non-quantized (Krifka 2001; Filip 2000).

Generally speaking, these oppositions capture the difference in interpretation that has been observed for sentences such as those in (6) below:

(6)   a. John ate.

        b. John ate mangoes.

        c. John ate a mango.

(6a–b) are interpreted as lacking an Endpoint (i.e. Atelic) due in this case to the lack of or inability of an internal argument which can constrain the event to a logical endpoint (cf. Tenny 1994). In contrast, (6c) is interpreted as containing a logical Endpoint due to the nature of the internal argument *a mango* which constrains the event to a logical Endpoint. This is so as the eating event must come to an end once the eating of *a mango* is complete.[2]

---

[2] Jackendoff (1996) develops and formalises the intuition behind the notion of "measuring out" (Tenny 1994) which I allude to here. He posits a representation of an event such that the affected object or theme is joined to a path; the telicity of the event depends not only on the nature of the theme but on the path. According to him,

> "[t]he position of the theme along the path is encoded as a function of time, so that for any arbitrary moment of time, there is a corresponding position [...] The theme is at the beginning of the path at the beginning of the event and at the end of the path at the end of the event. If the path has distinct segments, then the event can be divided into segments corresponding to when the theme is on the associated parts of the path" (p. 317–318)

1 Introduction

Examples such as those in (6) which show a particular verb appearing with different aspectual interpretations due to the influence of the internal argument establish the focus in aspectual analysis as minimally on the Verb Phrase (VP) as opposed to simply the aspectual properties of the verb. This viewpoint is summed up in Tenny & Pustejovsky (2000) who state that,

> [i]t is now generally accepted that we must talk about the aspectual properties of the verb phrase or the clause, rather than simply the aspectual properties of the verb since many factors including adverbial modification and the nature of the object noun phrase interact with whatever aspectual properties the verb starts out with (p. 6).

This statement is made in reference to developments in the field since Vendler's (1967); focus on the verb as a "crucial" factor in aspectual interpretation and his supposed division of verbs[3] into four classes: State, Activity, Accomplishment, and Achievement. Later reinterpretations of Vendler's verbal classes finally arriving at the basic State/Non-state distinction that we see for example in Verkuyl's (1996; 1999) use of the feature [+/−Change] point to a basic contribution of the verb to Aspect. Nevertheless, observations of the fact that a single verb may be used to express two different aspects due to the influence of the internal argument, (cf. Dowty 1979; Dahl 1981; Verkuyl 1996; Tenny 1994; MacDonald 2008, etc.) and also that different uses may be associated with a verb through context (cf. Tenny 1994: 4) make it logical to focus on VP as opposed to the aspectual properties of the verb.

1.5 Aspect in CECs and the nature of the verb

While this is accepted to be the case, the study of Aspect in CECs may benefit from further investigations into the nature of the verb itself and its contribution to Aspect. This is due mainly to discussions surrounding the large number of lexical items which may systematically express contrasting aspects; this behaviour is not necessarily due to the direct influence of internal arguments. If we consider the Jamaican Creole examples[4] in (7) and (8) below, we will see that the JC verb

---

[3]Vendler's classification has left some doubt as to whether or not it was based on just verbs or VPs due to his inclusion of both in his classification. Verkuyl (1999) for example points to this weakness in Vendler's classification, stating that: one can interpret him [Vendler] very benevolently as acknowledging the need to analyse aspectuality at the phrase level but in the meantime he made it impossible by distinguishing his classes at the verb level (p. 96).

[4]Please note that all JC examples, except where otherwise attributed, are from the author's own native speaker introspection.

1.5 Aspect in CECs and the nature of the verb

iit 'eat' is able to express either Telicity or Atelicity consistent with a change in the semantic denotation of the internal argument. In contrast, *redi* 'ready' seems to express opposing aspects based on the structure in which it appears:

(7) JC
   a. Jan **iit** mango.
      John eat mango
      'John eats mangoes.' (Habitual-Atelic)
   b. Jan **iit** tuu mango.
      John eat two mango
      'John ate two mangoes.' (Telic)

(8) a. Jan **redi** di pikni.
      John ready ART child
      'John readied the child.' (Telic)
   b. Di pikni **redi**.
      ART child ready
      'The child is ready.' (Atelic)

There are varying analyses on the contrasting Telicity that may be associated with a verb like 'eat' as shown in (7). First, there is a general view that points to the contribution of the internal argument in terms of the feature of specificity or finiteness (see authors such as Garey 1957; MacDonald 2008; Tenny 1994; Verkuyl 1996; 1999, etc.). Others though accepting the general idea of a relationship between the verb and its internal argument as responsible for the establishment of Telicity are divided on how this works within a compositional framework. Thus, for example, authors like Jackendoff (1996), and Krifka (1998) emphasise the relationship between the verb and its object as determining Telicity as opposed to a particular semantic feature contributed by the object. For such authors, (7) is not Telic simply because there is a specified internal argument, but because of the intrinsic relationship that is established between a verb like 'eat' and its internal argument whereby the internal argument provides a path, where for each part of the event of eating a sub-portion of the object is covered.

Focus on the relationship between the verb and its object rather than on a particular semantic feature of the verb allows for generalisation over different types of verbs. Such an approach takes into consideration the fact that verbs of motion such as *carry* behave differently as it relates to the relationship between the verb and its object (Object to Event (OTE) mapping) (see Krifka 1998; MacDonald

1 Introduction

2008; Tenny 1994). In another approach, Bennett & Partee (2004) articulate the view that the difference in interpretation in (2) (recalled below as 9) is due to the "ambiguity of the verb [...] and not the change in direct object" (p. 72).

(9) (adapted from Lyons 1977: 707)
 a. She **has** a headache. (Stative)
 b. She **is having** a headache. (Non-stative)
 c. She **is having** one of her headache. (Non-stative)

Such approaches which generally speaking may be said to focus the semantic contribution of different elements may be contrasted with the "exo-skeletal" approach articulated by Borer (2005) where the focus is on syntactic structures as providing "unambiguous formulas for the semantics to interpret" (p. 11).

1.6 A note on the compositionality of Aspect

In this work, I am inclined to accept an analysis which focuses on the relationship between the verb and its internal argument and the semantic contribution of both these elements within the context of Aspect as compositional. This viewpoint though relevant is however outside the specific scope of the discussion that I undertake in this study where as indicated, my focus is on the verbal component in Aspect. Given this, we note in the case of (7) and (8) above that there is indeed a difference in the Telicity indicated by the verbs in question. Loosely speaking, the difference in interpretation of the examples in (7) may be attributed to a difference in the type of internal argument, but the same may not be said of the examples in (8).

In the case of the verb *iit* in (7) both instances of the verb indicate Non-stativity (i.e.: Change); whether or not an Endpoint is established depends (in this case) on the semantics of the internal argument. In (7a) we note that the internal argument *mango* 'mangoes' is not specified as it relates to number or what has been called finiteness (Verkuyl (1996) or the feature "Specified Quantity of A" or [+SQA] (Verkuyl 1996; 1999; also Krifka 1998). The result of this interaction between the verb *iit* 'eat' and a non-finite internal argument is a predicate that is Atelic. In (7b) by contrast, the internal argument *tuu mango* 'two mangoes' is specified for number and the result is a predicate with a logical endpoint (Telic). Thus the difference in this aspectual interpretation (Telicity) may generally speaking be attributed to the contribution of the internal argument.

1.7 Dual aspect and the Stative/Non-stative distinction

A difference in interpretation is also noted for the examples in (8). However, in these cases, there is a difference in the structure of the sentence. In (8a) where *redi* 'ready' is used transitively it indicates a Change of state while in its intransitive use (8b) the default interpretation is that of a State. A lexical item such as *redi* 'ready' falls within the general group of items in CECs called "property items" (Migge 2000; Winford 1993), "predicate adjectives" (Seuren 1986) or "adjectivals"[5] (Kouwenberg 1996; also Sebba 1986). These include a range of items which to varying degrees may express what I call "dual aspectual" behaviour. This is in reference to the observation of their aspectual behaviour where in one instance they may express the feature Change[6] but yet in another express no Change. Items such as *sik, weeri, redi, braad* etc. which may be translated as either the adjective (sick, weary/tired, ready, broad) or inchoative verb (BECOME "get" sick, weary/tired, ready, broad) and also transitive verb (CAUSE to BECOME sick, weary/tired, ready, broad) have been of interest in CECs for some time now, starting perhaps with Voorhoeve (1957).

The descriptive reality where a single item may appear in different uses raises for many the theoretical question of the categorial status of such items. Are there several lexical entries for an item based on the categories in which it appears or can a single lexical item which allows for derivation into other categories be posited? The way in which this question is answered has implications for our understanding of the overall syntactic and semantic behaviour of such items and as such is a question to be considered carefully. The approach that is reflected in the literature is one that presents a unified position where "property items" are treated as either verbs (Alleyne 1980; Jaganauth 1987; Sebba 1986; Winford 1993; etc) or adjectives (Seuren 1986), or a combination of both verbs and adjectives (Kouwenberg 1996).

---

[5] Of these terms, I adapt that of "property items" in an effort to avoid as a focal point the discussion which centres on the categorial status of these items. As I point out in Chapter 3, the major focus in terms of these items has been their categorial status. While I contribute to this discussion in Chapter 6 of this work, I do this from the perspective of their aspectual status.

[6] This semantic concept is identified in Chapter 4 as the basic semantic feature within the Stative/Non-stative opposition. It is elaborated in Chapter 4 as simply Change in terms of MOTION, CHANGE OF STATE or CONTACT or any combination of these.

1 Introduction

Underlying this discussion of categorial status is the question of the aspectual status of this group of items and the Stative/Non-stative distinction.[7] In essence, given the fact that there is a group of items which appear in both Stative and Non-stative use, what then is the validity of the Stative/Non-stative distinction and can this be applied at the level of the verb? In this work, taking a basic "semantics prior" position where it is believed that the syntactic behaviour of a lexical item may be predicted by its semantic description (cf. Dixon 1977; also Levin 1993), I will tackle the question of the aspectual (status) behaviour of CEC property items from the perspective of lexico-semantic representations of verb meaning and primitive Event Structures.

Event Structure is used here in a sense similar to that of Pustejovsky (1988; 1991), in which Event Structure captures the most basic semantic information that the verb contributes to Aspect. This in turn predicts the different syntactic uses in which a lexical item may appear. Event Structure is "recursively defined in syntax" Pustejovsky (1991: 55), which means that it is affected by and redefined by the influence of other factors in the syntax. It is in this regard for example that MacDonald (2008) indicates in the case of verbs like *carry* that "a goal PP alters the [Event Structure] of a predicate i.e.: it turns an activity into an accomplishment"[8] (p. 6). Nevertheless, at the level of the verb the basic opposition established in the Stative/Non-stative distinction may be seen in the definition of the notions of State (Stative) on one hand and Process and Transition (Non-stative) on the other (ibid, p. 56). Regarding these, Pustejovsky (1988) defines a State as "an eventuality that is viewed or evaluated relative to no other event" (p. 22). A Transition is seen as "a single eventuality evaluated relative to another single eventuality" (p. 22). While a Process is "a sequence of identical eventualities" (p. 23)

---

[7]This distinction has been central in the discussion of TMA systems in Creole languages. In particular it has been used to account for the observed difference in the Tense interpretation of unmarked verbs in CECs where the unmarked Stative verb is interpreted as present while the unmarked Non-stative verb is interpreted as past (cf. Bickerton 1975; Winford 1993, etc). This discussion is highlighted in Chapter 2.

[8]Note that in my attempt to focus on the concept of a basic contribution of the verb to Aspect, I avoid the use of terms which directly include the interaction between the verb and other elements. Thus terms like Activity, Accomplishment, Achievement etc, are not used in reference to verbs and the inherent Event Structure with which they are associated. Such terms are however accepted with reference to the interaction between the syntax and the semantics at the level of inner aspect.

1.8 The proposal

I will argue that these so called property items in CECs constitute those items which are inherently State (Stative) and those which are inherently Transition (Non-stative). In establishing this, I look at not just the syntactic behaviour of these items (i.e.: whether or not they are compatible with Non-stative use either by compatibility with Imperfective aspect or transitive variation) but crucially the semantic behaviour that they exhibit. I note in particular that in Non-stative use at least three different interpretations are possible for property items. These are:

(10) a. A change of state interpretation within a logical opposition[9] of contrariety (cf. JC *di fuud a kuul* 'the food is cooling', *dem a kool di fuud* 'they are cooling the food'. This non-stative interpretation is taken as linking the opposition HOT:COLD whereby it is taken that some element of HOT was the original state of the item undergoing the Change of state (food).
    b. A change of state interpretation with a logical opposition of contradiction (cf. JC *di shuuz a blak* 'the shoe(s) is/are getting black' *dem a blak di shuuz* 'they are blackening the shoe(s)'.
    c. An ongoing/processual interpretation with no change of state (cf. JC *im a bad* 'He is misbehaving').

I argue that items displaying the semantic behaviour in (10a) are in essence Non-stative (Transition) predicates while those displaying behaviour consistent with (9b and 9c) are Stative predicates derived to express Non-stativity (Change of state and Process respectively). The latter items are characterized by the same Event Structure as items which do not appear in Non-stative use. But, are distinct in that they are vulnerable to a morphological process that allows for the introduction of meaning components associated with Non-stativity (i.e.: CAUSE, BECOME and DO[10]).

An evaluation of property items from the perspective of their aspectual status and Event Structure projects logically into a discussion of the categorial status of these items. Consistent with the variation in aspectual behaviour that is displayed by these items, I posit a diverse categorisation including both (Stative) adjectives and (Change of state) verbs. Also, consistent with the derivation of Stative items to express Non-stativity, I observe that base adjectives may be derived into (Non-stative) verbs. Likewise, Non-stative verbs may be derived as

---

[10]I discuss these as notions associated with the expression of Change in Chapter 5, §5.4.

1 Introduction

(Stative) adjectives. This accounts for the Non-stative use of JC items such as *blak* 'black' and *red* 'red' as well as *jelas* 'jealous', *bad* 'bad', and the Stative use of items such as *raip* 'ripen', *mad* 'madden', *sik* 'sicken', etc.

In treating dual aspectual forms in CECs, I hope to directly address the contribution of the verb to Aspect within the context of a compositional approach to Aspect, which sees Aspect as comprising different elements apart from the verb. Based on this, Bickerton's (1975); Stative/Non-stative distinction is reduced to the feature Change consistent with Comrie's (1976) definition and unambiguously applied to the verb at the lexical level. However, this notion of inherent aspect as the fixed semantic contribution of the verb is taken as a part of Aspect which is compositional at the syntactic level. The accomplishment of a reconciliation between aspect as a fixed concept at the level of the verb and Aspect as compositional is significant not only as it relates to the study of Aspect in CECs but to the study of Aspect more generally where there has been much debate on the compatibility of lexical approaches to Aspect and compositional approaches (see Rothstein 2004; Tenny 1994; Verkuyl 1999; etc.).

1.9 Aim and scope of this work

The primary aim of this work is to provide a model for the analysis of property items in CECs. In so doing I will seek to:

(11) a. provide an account of the existence of lexical items which show dual aspectual behaviour
   b. elucidate the Stative/Non-stative distinction and how this may be applied in the context of dual aspectual items
   c. lend insights into the discussion surrounding the categorial status of property items based on the aspectual behaviour observed

In order to facilitate a categorisation of property items, I will examine the aspectual behaviour of a range of these in JC for a language-specific categorisation. I will use Winford's (1993) classification of property items based on Dixon's (1977) semantic classes as a point of departure. However, I will attempt to provide a classification that is based on aspectual behaviour rather than semantic concepts. For this I will apply the standard syntactic tests of compatibility with Progressive aspect and transitive alternation that have been used in the literature to test for Stativity (see for example Jaganauth 1987 and Winford 1993). These will however be accompanied by semantic criteria linked to different event types, and on the type of interpretation that arises where such an item appears in Non-stative use.

1.9 Aim and scope of this work

Due to the variation in the behaviour of these lexical items across CECs and even across varieties of the same Creole, it would be overly ambitious to say the least, to attempt a classification that would account for all CECs. This is consistent with Kouwenberg (1996) who notes that "there is too much variation across Creole languages to attempt a single explanation with cross-Creole validity" (p. 9). Nevertheless, the model that I provide which is based on primitive event types or Event Structures and the overall aspectual (i.e. syntactic and semantic) behaviour displayed by property items, will allow for generalisations to be made regarding the possible behaviour that may be observed for property items across Creoles.

The focus of this study is the contribution of the verb to Aspect. However, this is taken within the context of the compositionality of Aspect which I acknowledge in this work. In particular, as it relates to terminology, I identify three separate yet interacting levels of Aspect starting with the verb (inherent aspect), its interaction with arguments (inner aspect) and its interaction with grammatical aspect (outer aspect). In this regard, this is perhaps the first piece of work in the field of Creole studies that overtly addresses the compositionality of Aspect in these languages. The major terms may be summarised as follows:

(12) a. INHERENT ASPECT: This refers to the contribution of the verb to Aspect. It is captured in the State/dynamic distinction as defined by Comrie (1976) separating verbs which include "necessary change" from those which do not. However, while this usage has been extended to classifying not just verbs but phrases and propositions, I apply the distinction strictly to verbs that express Change from those which do not. Comrie's distinction is treated as analogous to the Stative/Non-stative in Creole studies as articulated by Bickerton (1975; 1981/2016).

b. INNER ASPECT: This points to the level of the syntax-semantics interface where the verb interacts with its argument(s) and also goal adverbials or Prepositional Phrases (PPs). At this level the contribution of the verb which I identify as [+/−CHANGE] interacts with the semantic contribution of the internal argument. Also, adverbial modifications in the form of a goal introduced through PP operate here in the establishment of an Endpoint. The relevant distinction here is captured in the Telic/Atelic opposition which underlies the concepts such as Achievement and Accomplishment on one hand, and Activity on the other.

c. OUTER ASPECT: This refers to the contribution of grammatical aspect. This concerns whether a situation is viewed in its totality as a "complete whole" or not (i.e.: The Perfective/Imperfective distinction, Comrie 1976) or not. Outer aspect is separated from inner aspect and inherent aspect as viewpoint aspect which is the subjective way in which a situation may be viewed by a speaker (Klein 1994; Smith 1983; 1991).

Regarding these levels of Aspect (12b–c) may be separated from (12a) based on the fact that they refer to structural levels of Aspect and the interaction between both semantic and syntactic information. As indicated, the area of inherent aspect will be my primary focus, however the terminology outlined here is consistent with a view of Aspect as compositional. In this regard, the separation of terminology is a key element in the understanding of the complex and multi-layered facets of aspect.

My hope is for an overall treatment of Aspect in CECs which takes into consideration the specific contribution of all the key elements involved within a compositional model. The treatment of the semantic contribution of the verb is only one step in that direction but crucial nonetheless as it advances the theoretical question of the *how* of compositionality. As Dowty (2006) indicates regarding the discussion of compositionality in language, "[this] really should be considered "an empirical question". But it is not a yes-no question, rather it is a "how"-question." (p. 5). Indeed, an exploration of such a central element as the verb and its contribution to Aspect will raise questions as to how it is that this element may be associated with an inherent aspectual value when the aspectual behaviour of such an item indicates aspectual flexibility. Nevertheless, with the assumption of compositionality, it is expected that the specific contribution of each participating element will be understood in an effort to analyse the different interactions that exist between and among the various elements involved. It is in this regard that Verkuyl (1999) points out that:

> Although people in general seem to adhere to the idea of a compositional approach, many of them do not take the consequences …that should be drawn: To find out which basic semantic material underlies aspectual composition and how the composition proceeds at higher phrasal levels (p. 16).

The work I undertake in this study should be seen as one step along this path. It will address issues surrounding the contribution of one element to Aspect in CECs, however this must be taken as a part of the whole rather than an attempt to address Aspect overall.

One limitation of this study is the focus on JC for a language specific classification. Generally speaking, this is indeed a limitation in that descriptions of specific CEC languages are way overdue especially in the area of Aspect. Nevertheless, the primary aim of this study is the establishment of a descriptive model based on universal properties of language to account for the behaviour of CEC property items and in particular "dual aspectual" items. Rather than a focus on whether or not an item falls within a specific category, the main concern is an explanation of why items are able to display the behaviour that they do.

Thus, while the study posits a language specific classification of "property items" for JC, this must be taken as no more than an exemplar of a classification, as even a complete classification for JC would have to consider different varieties of JC – something this study does not undertake. In short, this study provides a model for a descriptive analysis for CEC property items and hopefully property items in general.

1.10 The organisation of the work

The work is organised as follows: In Chapter 2, I will present an overview and discussion of relevant work that has been undertaken on Aspect in CECs. Starting with Voorhoeve (1957), I note among the works surveyed that very few have been concerned with Aspect on its own but rather aspect as it relates to Tense. Even then, the focus has been mainly on grammatical aspect markers and how these interact with different verbs. However, Bickerton's (1975); work on Guyanese Creole (GC) which points to the Stative/Non-stative distinction as "crucial" in the understanding of Tense-Aspect in Creole languages, if nothing else triggered much debate in later works. In particular, we see where questions have been raised regarding the unique aspectual status of verbal forms in light of items which appear in contrasting aspectual uses.

Chapter 3 will focus on the case of dual aspectual forms and the issues or problems associated with these in CECs. I point out that these items have mainly been treated from the perspective of the question of their categorial status and present the work of authors such as Sebba (1986), Seuren (1986) and Kouwenberg (1996) which represent different positions within this discussion. Regarding the question of the aspectual status of these items and the Stative/Non-stative distinction, I revisit data from Jaganauth (1987) to highlight the conceptual problem raised by items in her analysis. As a point of departure for an analysis of these items, I evaluate the work of Winford (1993), which is, to my knowledge, the most complete attempt to treat the group of property items from the perspective of aspect.[11] I highlight observational and explanatory inadequacies of this model pointing to the need for a different model that will account for the diversity of behaviour noted among these items.

---

[11]The later works of Winford (1997) and (2000) revisit this question but appear to lean on the basic insights from the initial (1993) analysis, hence the focus on this work here.

1 Introduction

Chapter 4 is an attempt to elucidate the Stative/Non-stative distinction and its application at the lexical level. In this chapter I reduce the notion of inherent aspect to the notion of Change, which separates verbs which express necessary Change (Non-stative) from those which do not (cf. Comrie 1976). I discuss the feature Change as indicated by different (combinations of) primitives such as what I call the initiators of Change (CAUSE and DO), and the primitive associated with inchoative Change (BECOME)[12] (see Dowty 1979; Carter 1988; McCawley 1968). Coming out of this chapter are the ideas that form the basis for the analysis that I present in Chapter 5.

In Chapter 5, I will present a model for the analysis of CECs property items. I outline a treatment that accommodates the range of semantic interpretations that may be associated with an item in Non-stative use. Thus items are not categorised as inherently Stative or Non-stative based on the fact that they appear in these uses but analysed from the perspective of an inherent Event Structure. I evoke Pustejovsky; Pustejovsky's (1988; 1991) notion of a Transition to account for items which express a Change from one state to another but which are interpreted relative to a logical opposition expressing a contrary in Non-stative use. Items within this category include JC *raip* 'ripe/become ripe/make ripe', *wet* 'wet/become wet/make wet', *sik* 'ill/become ill/make ill' *weeri* 'weary/become weary/make weary' among others.

I highlight items of this type as distinct from those that I label inherent States. Included among these are those which do not appear in Non-stative use such as JC *chupid* 'stupid', *sluo* 'slow', *nais* 'nice' etc. But there are also items within this category of State items which appear in Non-stative use, expressing either a Process event type or a Transition. Included here are items such as JC *bad* 'bad/misbehave', *jelas* 'jealous' (Process) and items expressing Colour such as *blak* 'black/become/make black' and *red* 'red/become red/make red' (Transition). With regard to these latter items, which display behaviours similar to that of Transitions, I observe the distinction whereby they do not appear to be linked to an overt logical opposition in the same way that inherent Transitions are. In particular, whereas an item such as *sik* 'sick' may be said to be linked to an overt logical opposition which is 'well' (SICK: WELL) in a relationship of contrariety, the observation for an item such as *blak* 'black' or *red* 'red' is that the opposition is less specific. Thus, a Change of state arriving at these simply means that the State did not hold previously. What is indicated is what did not hold hence an opposition such as BLACK: NOT BLACK or RED: NOT RED, a relationship of contradiction.

---

[12]Non-volitional Change in an internal argument.

1.10 The organisation of the work

For items such as these I present the argument that they are derived rather than inherent Transitions. These are arrived at through the introduction of relevant primitive components consistent with the interpretations that they allow, namely BECOME which accounts for the inchoative meaning and CAUSE which accounts for the causative meaning and the introduction of a Cause or Agent. Similarly, in the case of those State items which express a Process meaning, I argue for the introduction of the primitive DO which is associated with Agency.

Chapter 6 is a summary of the work with a focus on the implications for the analysis of the categorial status of the items in question. I observe for property items a diverse categorial status with the group consisting of both (Non-stative) verbs and (Stative) adjectives underlyingly. Consistent with the aspectual behaviour observed for these items, those items associated with an Event Structure of Transition and categorised as (Non-stative) verbs are shown to appear in verbal use or what I posit to be derived adjectival use. Such items are distinguished from those that I analyse as inherently associated with a State Event Structure and adjectival status. Although there are items in this class that may be derived to appear as (Non-stative) verbs, the semantic behaviour that these display in Non-stative use sets them apart from those that I analyse as inherent verbs. This analysis that I present diverges from what may be seen as the standard evaluation of these items as a monolithic group of either verbs or adjectives. It also specifically rejects the treatment of these items as Stative verbs.

2 Aspect in Caribbean English Creoles: An overview of works

2.1 Background

Aspect in Caribbean English Creoles (CECs) has been discussed in the context of descriptive studies focusing mainly on grammatical aspect markers and the interaction between these and different types of verbs. In this chapter, I will take a look at some of the work that has been undertaken on Aspect in CECs. Due to the plethora of work in the general area of Tense-Aspect in Creoles, it is hardly possible to mention all the works that might be relevant. However, the ones that I highlight in this discussion are those that may be credited with somehow having advanced the study of Aspect in CECs along the logical line of progression that I outline here.

The general progression of works may be said to have moved from being almost strictly concerned with grammatical aspect (see Alleyne 1980; Voorhoeve 1957) to the significance of inherent aspect (see Bickerton 1975; 1981/2016). Later on, questions about the validity of Bickerton's Stative/Non-stative distinction and its relevance to Creole studies (see Jaganauth 1987[1]) make way for more contemporary trends in analyses which are sensitive to the impact of various elements including inherent aspect, grammatical aspect, and also the issue of context (see Gooden 2008; Sidnell 2002; Winford 1993; 1997; 2000, etc.).

I focus on these works in this chapter to create a general background and context for the specific discussion that will be the primary concern of this work. As indicated in Chapter 1, this is the case of lexical items which display aspectual multi-functionality (dual aspectual forms) in that they may be used to express either Stativity or Non-stativity. The issues surrounding these items in my estimation are best reflected in the works of Alleyne (1980), Jaganauth (1987), and Winford (1993) which address the aspectual status of such items and also Sebba (1986), Seuren (1986) and Kouwenberg (1996) which focus on the categorial status

---

[1] There are many authors who have found fault with Bickerton's approach but have not focused so clearly on refuting the stative/non-stative distinction.

of these items. I focus specifically on the discussion in these works in Chapter 3. However, since these issues and the case of dual aspectual forms fall within the larger context of the discussion of Aspect in CECs, I will spend some time here looking at some of the principal works that have been undertaken in Aspect as a general area in CECs.

A review of the works indicated here will point to the general problem that I tackle in this work, i.e. the issue of the Stative/Non-stative distinction and its application in Creole studies. As we will see, based on current discussions in the field, it seems that most authors are willing to accept, to varying degrees, the impact of Stativity on temporal interpretation (see Gooden 2008; Sidnell 2002; Winford 1993; 2000). Nevertheless, the case of items that appear in both Stative and Non-stative use (see discussion of Jaganauth 1987 below) makes it difficult to commit to whether or not the feature Stativity is to be applied to the entire predicate or only to the head of the predicate, the predicator. Incidentally, this is true even of Bickerton (1975), who unexpectedly concludes that Stativity is to be applied to propositions after seemingly arguing for the distinction at the level of the verb (p. 30). Conversely, Gooden (2008) states that the feature Stativity is to be applied to the entire predicate, however, her tests for Stativity are applied to the verbs themselves effectively testing only inherent aspect.[2]

In the sections below I will highlight the main concerns of relevant works starting with Voorhoeve (1957).

2.2 Some contributions to the study of Aspect in CECs

2.2.1 Voorhoeve (1957)

Voorhoeve (1957) is one of the earliest works on Tense and Aspect in Creole studies. Its main concern is typical of many later works in the field in its focus on the semantic content of certain "prefixes"[3] occurring with verbal forms in Sranan (SR). He departs from what he calls the "translation" of SR into western Tense categories (p. 374) and was perhaps the first to note that forms such as *nati* 'to be wet' *hebi* 'to be heavy', *siki*, 'to be sick', *kba* 'to be ready', *nen* 'to be named', etc., are verbs (rather than adjectives) in SR. This he observes based on

---

[2] Although Gooden (2008) proposes the treatment of the Stative/Non-stative distinction as "a feature of the lexical aspect of the verb" (p. 315) her discussion effectively conflates this with inner aspect which includes the internal argument of the verb (cf. Verkuyl 1999).

[3] "Prefixes" here refers to grammatical Tense-Aspect markers, generally referred to in later works as preverbal particles

2.2 Some contributions to the study of Aspect in CECs

their ability to "combine with prefixes and to link ... with other words" (p. 377). Highlighting this, he points out:

> Many of these verbs are translated into European languages by means of adjectives and this is the reason why in the existing grammars of Sranan they are wrongly considered as adjectives. (p. 376–377).

He points out further, regarding the behaviour of a form such as *siki*, that this can be "a noun (meaning: sickness), an adjective (meaning: sick), an intransitive verb (meaning: to be sick), and a transitive verb (meaning: to make ill)" (p. 377). Voorhoeve's observation of this phenomenon was perhaps the base for later discussions on the status of such items. Regarding these, I will note in Chapter 3 that that discussion has taken two forms, namely the question of the status of these as either verbs or adjectives, and the question of (inherent) Stativity. In this work, I address both questions pointing out that whereas a number of authors have focused on the categorial status of such items, a discussion in terms of aspectual status provides an informed basis on which to resolve the issues, and should therefore be the starting-point.

In terms of grammatical aspect, Voorhoeve identifies the prefix *e*- as a marker of aspect in SR and determines this as "the indicator of the *non-completive aspect*" (p. 378). This marker is juxtaposed against the "unprefixed form" or what is known as the bare or unmarked verb which, according to him "indicates *the completive aspect*" (p. 378). The data he provides shows forms occurring both in the bare (unprefixed) form and prefixed by the aspectual marker *e*- (Table 2.1).

Having identified the marker *e*- as generally expressing Non-completive aspect, Voorhoeve observes further, based on data such as shown here, that this form is an indicator of "an imperfective, an iterative, a durative, a progressive and an inchoative aspect." (p. 378).

For Voorhoeve, however, "Non-completive" serves as an umbrella term for Imperfective, Durative, Progressive and Inchoative. He points out that: "All these mutually different values have in common that the action is considered independent of the result." (p. 378). In the case of unmarked verbs, he points out that "it is the unprefixed form which reveals the result of the action." Hence, the notion "Completive" (p. 378). Note here that Voorhoeve does not make allowance for different types of verbs in his approach, but focuses on the overall grammatical outlook that is indicated through the interaction between the verb and marker. Thus for him, the marker *e*- is associated with different aspectual values based on the meaning that is denoted in its varying occurrences.

2 Aspect in Caribbean English Creoles: An overview of works

Table 2.1: Verbs in bare form and prefixed by *e-* in Sranan (Voorhoeve 1957: 377–378)

Bare verb	Prefixed by preverbal *e-*
a dede he is-dead	*a e- dede* he dies
*a santi **kba*** the sand is-ready	*a santi **e-kba*** the sand gets-ready it has been nearly cleared away (from the truck)
*a watra **trubu*** the water is-troubled	*a watra **e-trubu*** the water becomes-troubled
*a **dip**i tumsi* it is-deep too-much	*a e- **dip**i tumsi* it gets-depth too-much
*mi **wan** waka* I want to walk	*m **e-wan** waka* I want-generally to walk
*i m'a **kan** was a kros dj i* your mother can wash the clothes for you	*i m'a **e-kan** e -was a kros dj i* your mother can-all-the-time continue-to-wash the clothes for you
*i no **sab** j a mon e-du kon* you not know how the money actually comes	*i n **e-sab** j a mon e-du kon* you not know-all-the time how the money actually comes
*a **sabi** pasi kba* he knows the road already	*a **e-sabi** pasi kba* he begins–to-know the road already
*pe Srnaman **de** j a moro prisiri* where Surinam-people are you have more fun	*pe Srnaman **e-de** j a moro prisiri* where Surinam-people are–ever you have more pleasure (fun)

It may be possible, however, to label the marker *e-* as simply a marker of Imperfectivity meaning that it focuses on different phases of the situation (Comrie 1976) while the unmarked verb indicates Perfectivity (i.e. focuses on the situation as a whole). Returning to the data above, we observe some consistencies in

2.2 Some contributions to the study of Aspect in CECs

the interpretation of the marker *e-* with the different verbs: We note that *e-* is consistent with the meaning 'become' or 'get' in the case of *dede* 'to die', *kba* 'ready', *trubu* 'troubled', *dipi* 'deep' signaling the initiation of a Change of state, i.e. an inchoative. Elsewhere, with verbs like *wan* 'want', *sabi* 'know', *de* 'to be' and modals such as *kan* 'can' we see a meaning akin to 'generally', 'always' or 'all the time', consistent with the Habitual. Further, with a verb like *was* 'wash', we see the meaning of 'to continue' which is consistent with the Progressive. In spite of the fact that all these meanings fall under the abstract category of Non-completive or, after Comrie (1976), Imperfective, a question that logically arises is whether there is something in the meanings of these different types of verbs that allows for the differing aspectual interpretations in each case.

This kind of data indicates that there are at least three different types of verbs, consistent with the different types of Imperfective meanings that arise. In particular, items of the type *dede* 'dead', *kba* 'ready', *trubu* 'troubled', *dipi*, 'deep' etc. seem to be what I call Change of state predicates which may be used to express Stativity as in the (a) examples and Non-stativity as in the (b) examples. In the presence of Imperfective aspect marking a Change of state is overtly indicated consistent with the meaning BECOME, a primitive concept associated with Change in lexico-semantic representations.[4] I will discuss items of this type in Chapter 5 but at this stage it suffices to say that such items seem to behave differently from others, as it relates to Imperfective aspect marking and the meaning that they denote in this respect. As we see here in relation to Sranan, the meaning indicated by items such as *wan* 'want', *sabi* 'know', *de* 'to be', and others such as the modal *kan* 'can' and *was* 'wash', is consistent with a Habitual and a Progressive, respectively.

In terms of a classification of verbs, Voorhoeve's approach may be said to be aimed at unifying the different classes of verbs in that he does not attempt any clear classification based on aspectual behaviours. As it regards verbs such as *nati* 'to be wet' as opposed to *waka* 'to walk', however, he notes that the un-prefixed form of verbs such as *waka* agrees with what he calls the "occidental perfect" while *nati* corresponds with the "occidental present". Regarding such a difference, he points out that:

> It is understandable that it is the verbs like *nati* (to be-wet), *nen* (to be-called), *abi* (to have) *de* (to be), etc., where the unprefixed form agrees with an occidental present, whilst the unprefixed form of verbs like *waka* (to walk) agrees with an occidental perfect. This is because the former in our language only indicate a state of being and possess a completive meaning. (p. 378–379)

---

[4]This is further elaborated in Chapters 4 and 5.

2 Aspect in Caribbean English Creoles: An overview of works

Though rudiments of a distinction between Statives and Non-statives can be discerned here, Voorhoeve makes no overt reference to universal inherent aspectual properties. Instead, he treats the differences in Tense interpretations between a bare verb like *nati* and *waka* as "understandable" or something that is natural based on the language-specific meanings of these items.

Overall, Voorhoeve's work brought into focus that it is not sufficient to analyse Creole languages based on English glosses. In particular the fact that words such as *nati* 'wet', *hebi* 'heavy', *siki* 'sick' may be interpereted as shown; constitutes a significant difference in the way that a Creole such as SR treats these items as opposed to their treatment in European languages. The aspectual categorization and status of similar items will be the topic of Chapter 5.

2.2.2 Alleyne (1980)

Alleyne may be said to adopt a similar approach to Voorhoeve (1957) in that both strive to unify the different types of verbs and focus primarily on grammatical aspect. Alleyne (1980) examines data from Guyanese Creole (GC), Jamaican Creole (JC), Krio, Saramaccan (SM), Sranan (SR) and Gullah (GU) for peculiarities of particular languages within this group. With regard to the expression of Tense Mood Aspect (TMA) grammatical markers, he notes that "[t]he basic structure of the verb phrase is remarkably uniform across the languages and dialects[5] under consideration" (p. 77). In this regard he points out that:

> Verb phrases characteristically have particles preposed to the predicate and by their occurrence, absence or combination express aspect, tense and mood (imperative and conditional). (p. 80)

With specific regard to Aspect, Alleyne's work attempts a general description of Aspect through evidence from grammatical aspect. His basic opposition is between Perfective and Non-perfective, where Habitual and Progressive are subcategories of Non-perfective. According to him,

> aspect is part of the basic structure of the verb phrase in all but imperative sentences. All dialects have two aspects: perfective and nonperfective. (p. 82).

He notes that the Perfective is unmarked in all dialects, while the Non-perfective takes different forms depending on the dialect and its ancestry (p. 82). The

---

[5]Note that Alleyne utilises the term *dialects* in reference to Caribbean Creole languages – a practice which is no longer followed within the field.

2.2 Some contributions to the study of Aspect in CECs

data he provides includes verbs like *waak* 'walk', *go* 'go' and *si* 'see' as shown below in (1):

(1) Unmarked verbs as Perfective in Creoles (Alleyne 1980: 82)

    a. JC
       Mi waak.
       1SG walk
       'I have walked.'[6]

    b. GC
       Mi waak.
       1SG walk
       'I have walked.'

    c. GU
       Mi si əm.
       1SG see it
       'I have seen it.'

    d. SR
       Mi waka.
       1SG walk
       'I have walked.'

Here, Alleyne provides examples from different Creole languages to show the unmarked form of the verb indicating Perfective aspect. When it comes to verbs such as 'love', 'want', 'know' etc. he points out that there is nothing special about these and that the unmarked form indicates Perfective irrespective of what may be suggested by means of an English gloss. In this regard, he points out that:

> a group of verbs, the same in all dialects and languages concerned, have their perfective aspect form glossed in English by a "present tense". Thus *mi sabi* (zero marker and therefore perfective) is glossed in English as 'I know' [...] other verbs belonging to this group are *memba* 'remember', *wan* 'want' and *lob(i)* 'love' There is nothing "irregular" about these verbs. The forms cited above have perfective meaning in Afro-American,[7] irrespective of their English gloss. (p. 83)

---

[6] Also included: 'I (always, sometimes) walk' (Habitual) ditto for (2b and c) as well.
[7] What Alleyne refers to as Afro-American dialects includes the group of languages here referred to as CECs.

Alleyne does not provide examples for verbs like 'love', 'want' or 'know' in the Perfective but points to examples of these with the Imperfective aspect marker as shown below:

(2) (Alleyne 1980: 83)
   a. SR
      Mi e   sabi.
      1SG ASP know
      'I (always) know' or 'I begin to know.'
   b. SR
      Mi e   wan en.
      1SG ASP want it
      'I (usually) want it.'
   c. JC
      A   nuŋ mi a   nuo.
      FOC now 1SG ASP know
      'It's now that I am finding out.'

An Imperfective marker is shown occurring with verbs such as *sabi, wan* and *nuo* here translated as the English 'know' and 'want'. These are usually considered as Stative verbs in English and perhaps included in the discussion to show that they can and do co-occur with Imperfective aspect marking.[8] .

Alleyne also makes reference to preverbal *done*,[9] which he labels as a reinforcer of Perfective aspect. He points out that while Perfective aspect is unmarked everywhere, it "can in all dialects be recognized by its being optionally conjoined with a verb meaning 'finish', which acts as a kind of reinforcer of the perfective aspect." (p. 82). The status of *done* as a marker of Perfective aspect has been questioned, however, based on its focus on the completion of an event where Perfective focuses on the event as "a complete whole" (Comrie 1976). In this regard, *done* may be argued to be an indicator of perfect Tense which is compatible with completion. According to Comrie (1976):

---

[8] It is important to point out here that the co-occurrence of Imperfective aspectual markers (Progressive in particular) with Stative verbs (Vendler 1967) has not been observationally adequate even for English. Essentially, Imperfective aspect can interact with various verbs; where it does interact with Stative verbs, the interpretation may be different from that of Non-stative verbs (note in Table 2.1 above that in one meaning it is the onset of the situation that is indicated. The interaction between grammatical aspect and inherent aspect is discussed in Chapter 5. See also discussion of Sidnell (2002) below.

[9] This form is derived from the English 'done' in most if not all CECs.

the perfect looks at a situation in terms of its consequences and while it is possible for an incomplete situation to have consequences, it is much more likely that consequences will be consequences of a situation that has been brought to completion. (p. 64)

Alleyne's analysis of *done* and similar forms in other Creole languages brings into focus the ongoing discussion on the semantic content of grammatical markers. As seen here, Alleyne holds the unmarked verb as the indicator of perfectivity while *done* is seen as a reinforcer of this. So in other words, it is an additional but overt marker that reinforces what is indicated by the null marker. I will review other analyses of the unmarked verb and *done* in the discussion of Youssef (2003) later on.

Overall, Alleyne's focus seems to be on establishing grammatical aspectual viewpoint as independent of other factors such as the nature of the verb. Thus he focuses on the fact that a meaning such as Perfectivity may be applied to a verb regardless of any categorisation that may be associated with the verb itself. In his view, any unmarked verb is consistent with the aspectual category Perfective. This is a significant observation in Creole studies as it relates to Aspect. An analysis of the same type of data from the perspective of Tense would have revealed contrasts in the meanings of different verbs as it relates to the indication of Past and Present (compare Bickerton 1975 below). However, since grammatical aspect must be taken as a particular view of a situation, this view may be associated with a situation regardless of the inherent nature of the situation. This is actually the type of approach that I take in establishing terminology for different levels of Aspect. However, I am careful to note the interaction between the different levels. In the case of Alleyne, we may note that his discussion, being focused on grammatical aspect, simply treats the categories Perfective and Imperfective as semantic aspectual categories without taking into consideration other layers of Aspect and the interaction between them.

Such an approach must be recognised as limited in terms of a treatment of Aspect as a semantically complex area. However, like Voorhoeve (1957) Alleyne may be credited with a focus on Aspect without any distraction by Tense as we have seen elsewhere in the field (compare Bickerton 1975). In this treatment, Alleyne advances the observation that "aspect, which is always marked, is of more importance than tense in the verbal systems of these dialects." (p. 85). This is an important observation, since Aspect has traditionally fallen under the wider umbrella of TMA in the study of Creole languages with Tense being the main focus. Studies with a primary focus on Aspect rather than Tense may yield different and perhaps more insightful results.

2.2.3 Bickerton (1975)

Bickerton (1975) stands out as the work which first identifies the Stative/Non-stative distinction as important in the interpretation of the bare form (unmarked verb) in Creoles. In addressing the claim that Creole languages "use an invariant form of the verb in all contexts" (p. 27), he claims that although the stem form (i.e. the unmarked verb, without preverbal material) is very frequent in Creoles it "has several different and quite distinct functions" (p. 28). In relation to GC he points out clearly that:

> the functions of the stem form in the Guyanese system depend on the stative–non-stative distinction ... with non-statives, it signifies 'unmarked past' – that is a (usually) single action that happened at a moment in the past that may or may not be specified but should not predate any action simultaneously under discussion (p. 28).

We note here that Bickerton's analysis is from the perspective of Tense and the aspectual status of different verbs is used to account for (default) Tense interpretation. He points out that the stem form of Statives signifies 'non-past'. In contrast, Non-statives have to be marked by what he calls the continuative-iterative (also non-punctual[10]) marker to be interpreted in a similar way (p. 28). The examples below (3–5) are used to illustrate this:

(3) Bare Non-statives denote past single action (Bickerton 1975: 29)

    a. GC
       L_ **run** out
       'L_ ran out.'

    b. Me **run** out.
       1SG run out
       'I ran out.'

    c. All of them **hold on** pon me.
       all of 3PL hold on on me
       'Everyone held on to me.'

---

[10] We see a trend here where a marker is labelled based on the different aspectual meanings that may be associated with it in interaction with different kinds of verbs. This marker is also discussed in other works as the Non-completive or Non-perfective aspect marker (see Voorhoeve (1957) and Alleyne (1980), for example.)

2.2 Some contributions to the study of Aspect in CECs

(4) Bare Stative denotes present state (p. 29)
GC

a. Mi na **no** wai dem **a du** dis ting.
1SG NEG know why 3PL ASP do this thing
'I don't know why they are doing this.'

b. Di rais wok **get** mo iizia fi du bika tracta **a plau** am.
ART rice work get more easier to do because tractor ASP plough it
'Rice farming becomes easier to do because tractors do the ploughing.'

(5) "Continuative-iterative" *a* marks Non-stative as "non-past" (p. 29)
GC
Wi **a pak** am op hai laik haus an wi kaal di plees karyaan.
3PL ASP pack it up high like house and 3PL call ART place X
'We pile it up as high as a house and we call the place the threshing-floor.'

As we see from the examples here, Stative and Non-stative verbs, when evaluated from the perspective of Tense, establish a contrast in interpretation. In particular, the unmarked Non-stative verbs 'run' and 'hold on' in (3) are shown to indicate Past while the unmarked Stative *no* 'know' in (4a) is present. Also as Bickerton shows in (4b) and (5), the Present Tense interpretation in the case of Non-stative verbs arises in the presence of overt (Imperfective) grammatical aspectual marking using what he calls the "continuative-iterative" marker *a*.

An analysis from the perspective of grammatical aspect would no doubt have yielded different results. In particular, similar to what was observed above for both Voorhoeve (1957) and Alleyne (1980), all the unmarked verbs in the examples above (3–5) may be analysed as Perfective independent of whether or not they are Stative or Non-stative. The contrast from this perspective comes from the appearance of the Imperfective aspect marker which establishes some form of Imperfectivity. However, we must be reminded that Bickerton's preoccupation was with Tense interpretation and the role of the verb in this, as opposed to that of Voorhoeve and Alleyne which had to do with (grammatical) aspectual outlook. In this regard, while grammatical aspect may in a sense be established regardless of the type of verb, it appears in effect that a focus on Tense raises different concerns. In particular, as we observe from the examples in (4–4.2) above, there is a difference in the (default) Tense interpretation of the unmarked verb, dependent on whether it is Stative or not. However, there is no such contrast in the aspectual outlook indicated in these Items.

2 Aspect in Caribbean English Creoles: An overview of works

Bickerton's focus on Tense, as opposed to Aspect, ironically highlights a level of aspectual interpretation below that of grammatical aspect. This level, although not seemingly impactful in the case of the unmarked verb, assumes relevance in the case of Imperfective aspectual marking. In this regard, Bickerton observes a contrast in the behaviour of Stative and Non-stative verbs in the face of "continuative" (also Progressive or more generally Imperfective) marking. He points out that: "the occurrence of statives and continuative markers is as unacceptable as it is in English."[11] (p. 30). The examples below show this restriction:

(6) Bickerton (1975: 30)

    a. * mi a **nuo** da
        1SG ASP know that
        ('I am knowing that.')

    b. * dem a **gat** wan kyar
        3PL ASP have one car
        ('They are having [sc. possessing] a car.')

As shown here, the Stative verbs *nuo* 'know' and *gat* 'possess' are shown to yield ungrammatical utterances in their occurrence with the Imperfective aspect marker *a*.

Note though that a number of authors have since challenged the observational adequacy of this, showing the combination of Stative verbs and Imperfective aspect marking as well attested in CECs (see Jaganauth 1987; and Sidnell 2002 discussed below). Of interest, however, is the type of aspectual interpretation that may arise in the face of this combination. Sidnell (2002) for example, shows that the combination of Stative verb and Imperfective aspect marking has predictable constraints on meaning. In particular, with Stative verbs the interpretation is Habitual while Imperfective aspect marking with Non-stative verbs yields an interpretation that is Progressive (cf. data above in Voorhoeve (1957), where similar interpretations are shown for verbs like 'want' as opposed to 'wash'). This difference in aspectual interpretation suggests a need to further understand the impact of the verb in aspectual interpretation; or what exactly is responsible for such a difference in interpretation. This is one of the motivators behind the overall study that develops in this work.

---

[11] Compare with Vendler's (1967) observation of a restriction on the occurrence of Stative verbs with Progressive aspect. Recall also that this restriction has been challenged. I return to this in Chapter 5

2.2 Some contributions to the study of Aspect in CECs

Bickerton, even in his very definitive stance on the Stative/Non-stative distinction as crucial in Creoles, was not very clear on its theoretical application. Although his general discussion indicates that he applies the Stative/Non-stative distinction to verbs, in addressing items such as those in (7) which seemingly appear in both Stative and Non-stative use, he indicates an application of the distinction to propositions rather than to verbs. Compare:

(7) Bickerton (1975: 30)

    a. Tu an tu **mek** fo.
       two and two make four
       'Two and two make four.'

    b. Dem **mek** i stap.
       3PL make it stop
       'They made him stop.'

As observed here, the form *mek* appears in both Stative and Non-stative use being expressed as the equivalent of the English Stative verb *to be equal to* in (7a) and the causative Non-stative *cause* in (7b). In following through with his observation of default Tense interpretations for Stative and Non-stative verbs, Bickerton observes that *mek* in (7a)

> follows the rule for stative verbs (stem-only for non-past)" [while 7b] "has a non-stative meaning and in it, *mek* must therefore follow the non-stative rule (stem-only for simple past) (p. 30).

Based on examples such as (7), Bickerton states explicitly (perhaps rather unexpectedly) that

> the stative-non-stative distinction in Guyanese Creole is a semantic one entirely: That is to say, it is not the case that specific lexical items are marked unambiguously [+stative] or [−stative], rather that these categories apply to propositions irrespective of their lexical content. (p. 30)

We note here that Bickerton applies the Stative/Non-stative distinction to propositions rather than to lexical items. However, notice even here that it is the verb that is then associated with the feature [+/− Stative] on the basis of the proposition in which it appears. Thus, while he notes a Stative *meaning* for the proposition in (7a), he still applies this to the verb itself, as he points out consequently that "*mek* must therefore follow the non-stative rule (stem-only for simple past)" (p. 30). So the question still is whether or not the Stative/Non-stative distinction for him is applied to propositions or verbs.

His statement that the application is to propositions rather than lexical items seems contrary to his actual approach where it is lexical items that are called on for observation and application of the distinction. However, what we note here is a genuine difficulty in associating a form with lexical specification and actual use. Thus in this case, the differences in meaning suggest that we are dealing with two different forms altogether rather than a single form associated with different realisations and consequently different meanings.[12] *Mek* in (7a) functions as a main verb with a meaning that points to a generic (logical) result with no indication of Change (i.e.: the equivalent of the English form with the meaning 'to be equal to') while *mek* in (7b) is an overt causative verb indicating and introducing an initiator CAUSE in a Change of state.

While this difference in what appears as a single lexical item is evident from a perspective which distinguishes forms based on meanings, it is not so evident if the focus is principally on the form. Thus, from Bickerton's perspective, based on the differences observed in the instantiations of *mek*,

> one must either arbitrarily list mek_1 [+stative] and mek_2 [−stative] in the lexicon, or one must admit that the syntactic component can somehow "read" semantic information, i.e. that semantics is generative rather than interpretive. (p. 30)

Bickerton here appears to find the prospect of an "arbitrary" listing in the lexicon of two different *mek* as uneconomical. For him, in the case of *mek* we are dealing with one lexical item distinguished only by the feature Stativity. However, indications based on the meaning components associated with the form in each instance, are that we are indeed dealing with different semantic forms. The case of mek_1 being a verb with the associated meaning 'to be equal to' and mek_2 is the causative verb indicating an initiator in a Change of state.

While the case of *mek* appears here as a case of homophony, a real challenge to Bickerton's Stative/Non-stative distinction is the case of those items which appear indeed as single lexical items in both Stative and Non-stative uses. If we interpret Bickerton benevolently, it would be fair to say that his approach to

---

[12] Compare to items that I treat as dual aspectual forms in Chapter 5. These are different from the case of *mek* in that they feature single lexical items in different uses and the uses are linked to a single abstract Event Structure which accounts for both uses.

the Stative/Non-stative distinction has been made somewhat unclear with his indication that it is to be applied to propositions; pointing to more than just the verbs but treating verbs based on the propositions that they can appear in. In the approach that I follow in this work, the notion of Stativity is reduced to the semantic concept of Change and applied directly to lexical items even in the context of dual aspectual forms.

Bickerton's work, starting with this (1975) work may be credited with the glut of work on TMA in Creole languages due to his insistence on the importance of the Stative/Non-stative distinction to understanding Tense in Creoles. This impact is noted by authors outside of the field of Creole studies, who also credit Bickerton with the fact that Creole studies on TMA seem to exist in a world that is separate from the general theoretical genre. In this regard, Dahl (1993) for example notes that due to the impact of Bickerton's work,

> the study of Creole TMA systems has become an autonomous tradition, with its own terminology and conceptual apparatus with an ensuing relatively restricted influence on non-creolist TMA studies. (p. 251)

2.2.4 Bickerton (1981/2016)

In his 1981/2016 work, Bickerton again focuses on the Stative/Non-stative distinction which he now also refers to as the State-Process distinction (SPD), this time in relation to language acquisition. Regarding this distinction, he claims that it is "directly involved in the acquisition of the English Progressive marker -*ing*." (p. 138). He states that "just as there are verbs that do not take -*ed*, there are verbs that do not take -*ing*... such as *like, want, know, see*, etc." (p. 138). He points out that:

> These verbs are quite common in children's speech, probably as common as many of the irregular verbs to which children incorrectly attach -*ed*. Yet apparently, children never attach -*ing* to stative verbs (p. 138).

Based on this, he presumes the SPD to be innate "not because of its universality [...] but because it plays a crucial role in Creole grammars." (p. 142). Here again he points to differences in the behaviour and default interpretations of Statives as opposed to Non-stative verbs stating that,

> present-reference statives and present-reference nonstatives cannot be marked in the same way, and the same applies to past reference statives and non-statives (p. 142).

For this he provides the following table, which shows restrictions based on the SPD in GC (Table 2.2).

Table 2.2: Bickerton's (1981/2016: 142) model of GC Tense-Aspect

	Stative	Non-stative
Present Reference	∅	a
Past Reference	bin	∅

Similar to his observation in his 1975 work Bickerton shows here that an unmarked Stative verb by default is interpreted as present while the unmarked Non-stative is interpreted as past. To be interpreted with present reference, the Non-stative verb must be preceded by the Imperfective aspect marker (*a* in this case); the Stative verb must be preceded by the overt Past Tense marker *bin* in order to be interpreted as Past.[13] This analysis by Bickerton, like his proposal of a restriction on the occurrence of Stative verbs with Imperfective aspect marking, has been challenged by authors such as Jaganauth (1987), Winford (1993), and Gooden (2008), who point to the involvement of other factors that may affect the interpretation arising from these combinations.

Both Bickerton's (1975) and (1981/2016) works managed to provoke much debate with regard to Tense and Aspect expression but, as I pointed out, were not intended primarily to answer questions related to Aspect. What Bickerton (1975) did successfully, however, was to show that Creoles do indeed have a Tense system and that there is a systematic way in which this is expressed, depending on the type of verb and its inherent aspect.

2.2.5 Jaganauth (1987)

Jaganauth (1987) responds to Bickerton's claims regarding the Stative/Non-stative distinction and claims this as "empirically invalid" both in terms of Bickerton's predicted restrictions and default interpretations (p. 21). Along these lines, she provides data from GC that goes contrary to Bickerton's observations. In particular, she shows the occurrence of "so called" Stative verbs with the Imperfective aspect marker, as well as Stative verbs appearing with what she calls a dynamic verb interpretation, and also instances where it is unclear whether the

---

[13] This same marker is allowed with Non-stative verbs but the interpretation in such cases is that of Anterior or "Past before Past" as opposed to a simple "Past".

2.2 Some contributions to the study of Aspect in CECs

interpretation of a particular verb is Stative or Dynamic. The data below is set out along these lines:

(8) Stative verbs in Non-stative use (GC)

a. Somtaim mi a de gud, somtaim mi a sik.
   sometimes 1SG ASP be fine, sometimes 1SG ASP ill

   'Sometimes I would be enjoying good health, other times I would not.' (p. 23)

b. A now mi a no da.
   FOC now 1SG ASP know that

   'I am now discovering that.' (DYNAMIC) (p. 31)

c. I na bin a get non pikni.
   3SG NEG TNS ASP get NEG child

   'He wasn't succeeding in fathering (obtaining) any children.' (DYNAMIC) (p. 30)

d. I na **bin get** non pikni.
   3SG NEG TNS get NEG child

   i. 'He didn't have (possess) any children.' (STATIVE)

   ii. 'He didn't father any children.' (DYNAMIC) (p. 30)

(8a–c) shows the GC Stative verbs *de* 'be', *get* 'obtain' and *no* 'know' co-occurring with the Imperfective aspect marker *a*. (8d) shows what is indicated as by Jaganauth as the ambiguous interpretation of the item *get*. This data as indicated, serves partly to disprove Bickerton's (1975) observation regarding the Stative/Non-stative distinction and a restriction on the occurrence of the Imperfective marker with Stative verbs. With regards to the appearance of Imperfective aspect marking with Stative verbs, as I pointed out earlier, what is important in such cases is not just the fact that these elements co-occur but more so the aspectual meaning that arises. In particular, if we examine the data in (8), we note in the case of the verb *no* 'know' in (8b) for example that what is indicated is the onset of the situation as opposed to its progression - an interpretation associated with certain Non-stative verbs in interaction with Imperfective aspect marking. I discuss this interaction between Imperfective aspect marking and different types of verbs in §5.2.

Closer examination of (8a, c and d) also raises the question of what it means to be "Stative" and the inherent aspectual status of the items *de* and *get* as used here.

2 Aspect in Caribbean English Creoles: An overview of works

In the case of *get*, the meaning indicated in (8c) is one which includes Change[14] (obtain) and can be contrasted with *get* which indicates possession (8d i.); an inherent State based on the definition I posit in Chapter 4. Although, 'get' appears as a single lexical item on the surface, it seems that is expresses two meanings. The first a Change of state (obtain) and the second a State (possess) – possibly the result of the Change of state meaning, though not necessarily so. Such behaviour may be associated with the Event Structure of Transition (Pustejovsky 1988; 1991) as I discuss it in Chapter 4. This would account for the ambiguity in meaning that Jaganauth indicates for (8d) above. However, the use of the form in (8c) is clearly a Non-stative instantiation ('to father') and thus not the case of a Stative verb occurring with Imperfective aspect marking.

In the case of *de* the meaning content here would need to be further investigated. Jaganauth seems to analyse *de* here under the condition that it is the Stative (locative) form 'to be'. However, there appears to be a similar form *de* which rather than a locative (be), serves to introduce a stage level meaning in contrast to the individual level meaning that may be associated with the Stative (locative) *de*. Compare:

(9) (personal CEC data)

    a. Ai **de** ier.
       1SG COP here
       'I am here.' (I am just existing)

    b. Ai gud.
       1SG good
       'I am well/ok.' (generally)

    c. Ai **de** gud.
       Is COP good
       'I am well.' (at the moment)

As we see from these examples, *de* may express a location or a psychological state of mind as in (9a) but in (9c) it seems to introduce the meaning of Transitory State. We see this when we compare (9b) to (9c). In the case of (9c) as opposed to (9a), the predicate seems to be *de gud* which expresses a temporary State as opposed to *de* which expresses a more general State. When we further compare

---

[14] In Chapter 4 I elaborate the notion of Change as an abstract semantic notion. This is contained in the semantic representation of the verb and may be represented through primitives indicating a Change of state such as BECOME, and causation through the primitive CAUSE – all associated with Non-stativity.

(9c) with (8a) above which shows the presence of the Imperfective aspect marker, the meaning is one of progressivity – characteristic of a Non-stative verb in interaction with Imperfective marking.[15]

In addition to the cases discussed in (8), Jaganauth also points to data in the form of items such as *ded* 'to die, dead' and *fraikn* 'frighten, afraid' to highlight the ambiguity that may be associated with lexical items. Also the case of items such as *sik* 'ill, make ill', *weeri* 'weary, make weary', *redi* 'ready, make ready' etc. which also appear in both stative and Non-stative use. These are shown in (10) and (11) respectively:

(10) Stative verb occurs with dynamic or ambiguous Stative/Dynamic verb interpretation (GC) (Jaganauth 1987: 31–32)

   a. I **ded** siks a klak dis maanin.
      3SG dead six o'clock this morning
      'He died at six this morning.' (DYNAMIC)

   b. Now i **ded** dem kom bak.
      now 3SG dead they come back
      'Now that he is dead/has died they have returned.' (STATIVE/DYNAMIC)

   c. Mi **fraikn** a daag.
      1SG frighten a dog
      'I have scared the dog'. (DYNAMIC)

   d. Mi **fraikn** a daag.
      1SG frighten of dog
      'I fear/am afraid of the dog'. (STATIVE)

(11) GC (Jaganauth 1987: 31)

   a. Da tablit **sik** mi stomik.
      that tablet sick 1SG stomach
      'That pill has made me ill.'

   b. Dis baskit **weeri** mi.
      this basket weary 1s
      'This basket has made me tired'.

---

[15] I am not here suggesting that *de* has the function of a Non-stative verb but rather that the combination *de gud* introduces a meaning that is consistent with a more temporary State. The interaction between this kind of predicate and the Imperfective aspect marking provides a more Progressive type interpretation as opposed to the Habitual or inchoative that typically arises with Statives. See discussion of the interaction between the Progressive and different types of verbs in Chapter 5 (§5.2).

c. I **redi** shi.
   3SG ready 3SG
   'He has gotten her ready'.

As shown here, lexical items such as *ded* and *fraikn* appear in different instances associated with either the Stative meanings 'dead' and 'fear' or the Non-stative meaning 'to die' and 'to frighten' respectively. For the items in (11) we see these appearing in Non-stative use indicating a Change from one State to another with an obvious Cause or Agent. These may be compared to cases where these items appear in Stative use. Compare:

(12) (Personal JC data)

a. Mi stomik sik.
   1SG stomach sick
   'I am ill.'

b. Mi weeri.
   1SG weary
   'I am weary/tired.'

c. Shi redi.
   3SG ready
   'She is ready.'

Based on cases such as these Jaganauth claims that:

> there are instances [...] where it would be impossible to determine with any certainty whether the situation referred to is stative or dynamic.[16] (p. 35).

Jaganauth's argument for these is that the presence of an affected object rather than the fact that the verb is Stative or Non-stative accounts for the difference in aspectual interpretations. According to her

> it is the presence or absence of other elements in the proposition or the non-linguistic context which serves to focus on one or the other perspective of the situation (p. 35).

---

[16] Note here that Jaganauth applies the Stative/Non-stative distinction to propositions hence the difficulty in determining whether a sentence is Stative or Non-stative as all the elements in the sentence contribute to this. If the Stative/Non-stative distinction is applied to the verbs themselves, we will see that close examination of the meanings indicated by these verbs actually coincide with the feature Jaganauth applies to each of these sentences.

2.2 Some contributions to the study of Aspect in CECs

While I do agree with Jaganauth's observation of the involvement of other factors (outside of inherent aspect) in aspectual outlook, the concept of a basic primitive Event Structure associated with lexical items provide a way of capturing an inherent contribution of the verb to Aspect. Essentially, what Jaganauth calls the "the presence or absence of an affected object" is linked to a predicate's ability to express Change and thus related to (Non)-Stativity. In my treatment of items expressing similar behaviours, I link the behaviour of such items to a basic Event Structure template following Pustejovsky (1988; 1991). Thus for example items such as *ded* 'dead' and *fraikn* 'frighten' based on the behaviour that they display are linked to an Event Structure of Transition that includes Change and are thus Non-stative. Items of the type *ded* 'dead' which fall within the larger group of property items in CECs will be the focus of the discussion in Chapters 4 and 5 where I articulate a treatment.

In the case of *get* while I do not focus on forms of this type, it appears to represent the case of homonyms; a single form associated with distinct (though perhaps related) meanings. From this perspective as well, such forms may be associated with a status as Stative or dynamic based on the usage in which it appears. Thus where *get* appears with a meaning equivalent to 'possess' it would be an instantiation that is Stative and likewise, where the interpretation is 'obtain' it would be Non-stative. In this way, the aspectual status of a form is linked directly to the meaning associated with such a form and whether or not it expresses Change. This treatment is further elaborated in Chapter 5.

An analysis of the type which I articulate in this work, which, takes into consideration lexico-semantic representations and primitive meanings in the treatment of these lexical items may have provided Jaganauth with the tool to merge the idea of a unique aspectual contribution of the verb with the variable behaviour of items in her data. This is something that I attempt to do in this work.

Jaganauth's study, while noting the deficiencies in other accounts, cannot be credited with presenting a workable alternative. In summarizing, Jaganauth takes into consideration the involvement of several elements in aspectuality but fails to admit the contribution of the verb to aspectuality. The data that she provides in her study points to the necessity of a treatment of Aspect in CECs that acknowledges and treats the case of forms which express "dual aspectual" behaviour.

2.2.6 Winford (1993)

Winford (1993),[17] like Jaganauth (1987), acknowledges a certain superficiality in the nature of studies on TMA.[18] In this regard, Winford states that while the general facts about the CEC verb system are well known, they have been presented in a "rather piecemeal fashion and for the most part in informal terms" (p. 26). His work attempts to put the pieces together. Winford's approach, unlike that of Jaganauth, "preserves the simple intuition that certain predicators involve change or process while others do not" (p. 26). In other words he may be said to intuitively accept the Stative/Non-stative distinction. Like Bickerton (1975; 1981/2016) he points to a clear contrast in the interpretation of bare Non-stative verbs as opposed to Statives. This is shown below in (13) and (14) (Winford 1993: 33):

(13) CEC (Non-statives)

   a. Mieri **rait** wan leta.
      Mary write one letter
      'Mary wrote/has written a letter.'

   b. Jan **iit** di mango.
      John eat ART mango
      'John ate/has eaten the mango.'

(14) CEC (Stative)

   a. Di pikni **waant** waata.
      ART child want water
      'The child wants water.'

   b. Sam **lov** di uman fi truu.
      Sam love ART woman for true
      'Sam truly loves the woman.'

Regarding these, Winford points out that, "[a]s the translations suggest, the default interpretation of base non-stative verbs is "Past", while that of "statives" is "Present" (p. 34).

---

[17]Later works by Winford (1997; 2000) generally reflect sentiments similar to those highlighted in this section. These works, though not discussed here, are alluded to later in Chapter 3 where I deal with the problem of dual aspectual forms in the literature.

[18]These sentiments are repeated in his later works (1997) and (2000).

2.2 Some contributions to the study of Aspect in CECs

In his application of the Stative/Non-stative distinction, Winford rejects Bickerton's (1975) view that the Stative/Non-stative distinction applies to propositions rather than to specific lexical items. In treating the flexibility of interpretation that we observe in certain forms, however, he acknowledges difficulties in the application of the Stative/Non-stative distinction and, like Jaganauth (1987), points to the influence of other factors. According to him,

> [t]he stative/non-stative distinction is sometimes quite difficult to apply in practice for two reasons. First, there is the problem of the interaction between contextual influences and the "inherent meanings" of the verb. In many cases, predictions about the possible behaviour of, say, a "stative" verb turn out to be falsifiable, given the appropriate discourse context. Secondly … there is a great deal of flexibility in how individual verbs may be used (p. 29).

This statement shows sensitivity to the involvement of other factors within the context of the application of the Stative/Non-Stative distinction, namely the factor of discourse and the flexibility in the usage of verbs. The examples in (15) below, for example, show how the presence of adverbials conditions the interpretation of unmarked Statives:

(15) Trinidadian Creole (Winford 1993: 34–35)

    a. Ai **noo** hi wen hi juuzta liv bai hi faada.
       1SG know 3SG when 3SG used to live by 3SG father
       'I knew him when he used to live at his father's.'

    b. Ai **noo** hi moda in dem deez.
       1SG know 3SG mother in them days
       'I knew his mother in those days.'

    c. Ai **noo** hi moda fu a lang taim.
       1SG know 3SG mother for ART long time
       'I've known his mother for a long time.'

    d. Ai **noo** hi moda sins mi smaal.
       1SG know 3SG mother since 1SG small
       'I've known his mother since I was small.'

In comparison to the Stative verbs in (14) above, which are interpreted as present, we note that the interpretation of the Stative verb *noo* 'know' here is Past or Tense neutral. Winford attributes this to context, explaining in the case of (15a) that

> the context clearly establishes that the *hi* 'he' in question no longer lives at his father's, and that *noo* 'know' refers to a past acquaintance (p. 35).

With regards to (15b–d), he points to the influence of adverbials stating that such examples

> reinforce the view that Ø-marked statives can be neutral with respect to time reference, for which they rely on adverbial and other specification. (p. 35)

However, without such specification, he maintains that "the default reading of unmarked statives [...] is "Present"" (p. 35).

By accounting for such cases through the influence of factors such as context and the presence of adverbials, Winford establishes a treatment of Aspect that is sensitive to both primary and secondary interpretations. In essence, there is a default interpretation but context may allow for the possibility of another (secondary) interpretation. This is one of the most appealing features of Winford's approach. From this perspective it may be appropriate to say that he transcends his predecessors in not depending on any single element in his account. However, while his approach points to the involvement of different factors in Aspect in CECs, he does not provide a model that indicates how these factors interact to yield a particular aspectual outlook. In addition, it is not clear how the Stative/Non-stative distinction applies at the lexical level and how this works in relation to items which display aspectual flexibility.

2.2.6.1 Winford (2001)

Winford (2001) is more focused on a typological classification of CECs but he reinforces some of the points made in his 1993 work. In particular, he maintains that the Stative/Non-stative distinction is applicable in the aspectual systems of CECs and in this regard, he generalizes that "[t]he stative/non-stative distinction is crucial to the interpretation of temporal and aspectual meaning." (p. 5). He uses this distinction as a basis for the interpretation of Tense, indicating that unmarked Statives in the varieties under focus (SR, GC, JC and Belizean Creole (BC)) all signal "simple present" while unmarked Non-statives all signal "absolute past" (p. 5).

Regarding a typological classification of CECs he focuses on grammatical aspect and how CEC languages organise their systems around the Perfective/Imperfective distinction or the Progressive/Non-progressive distinction. According to him,

2.2 Some contributions to the study of Aspect in CECs

> [i]t is difficult to generalize about the typology of CEC aspectual systems. There seems to be a broad distinction between CEC's which organize their aspectual systems around the Perfective/Imperfective distinction (e.g., Sranan, rural Guyanese), and those that organise them around the Progressive vs Non-progressive distinction (e.g., Jamaican and Belizean) (p. 6–7)

Based on this, he characterises Sranan and rural Guyanese as "closure" languages while Jamaican and Belizean are "dynamicity" languages (p. 7). As can be seen here, the characterization of these languages is based on how the aspectual systems treat viewpoint aspect or grammatical aspect in overall aspectual outlook.

The main contribution of Winford's work may be said to be his effort to employ general theoretical models of Aspect in his description of CEC aspectual systems. His work overall has to be credited with finding a way to include inherent aspect in an analysis of Aspect within the context of the influence of other elements.[19] In this way, his work is one of the few which creates a basis for a holistic treatment of Aspect.

2.2.7 Andersen (1990)

Andersen's (1990) work on Papiamentu is worthy of note here as it effectively separates Aspect from Tense as an area of study in Creole languages establishing the marker *ta* that was previously analysed as Tense marker as a grammatical aspect marker.[20] He also points to the treatment of both "inherent semantic aspect" and "grammatically imposed aspect" as "useful as a framework to interpret the functional properties of the Papiamentu tense-aspect morphological system." (p. 66). His approach stands out as one that acknowledges the compositionality and complexity of Aspect.

Regarding inherent aspect, Andersen identifies the feature Stative as "very relevant to Papiamentu" (p. 66). In this regard, providing some support for Bickerton (1975), he points out that "most (but not all) Stative verbs in Papiamentu cannot be preceded by either the "present" Imperfective marker *ta* or the past Imperfective marker *a*. He also points to another group of Stative verbs that do allow for the Imperfective aspect marker. It is not clear what semantic restrictions allow for some Stative verbs to be preceded by the Imperfective aspect marker while

---

[19]This sensitivity to the variety of elements in involved in Aspect, allowed him to note in his earlier work (Winford 2000: 389) the compatibility of 'non-punctual' aspect with Statives.

[20]The interpretation of *ta* as an Imperfective aspect marker has been challenged by Kouwenberg & Lefebvre (2007)

restricting others. However, what this does suggest is that the picture is more complex than a mere restriction on the occurrence of Stative verbs with Imperfective grammatical aspect, and that the group of Stative forms may be more diverse than previously thought. Andersen's groups of Stative verbs are shown below in (16) and (17); groupings are based on their ability to be preceded by Imperfective grammatical aspect marking.

(16) Andersen's Stative verbs that do not allow grammatical marking by *ta* or *a* (p. 71)
   a. *ta* 'be'
   b. *tin* 'have, exist'
   c. *por* 'can, may'
   d. *sa* 'know (something)'
   e. *konosé* 'know (someone)'
   f. *ke* 'want'
   g. *mester* 'have to, must, should'
   h. *yama* 'be called'

(17) Stative verbs that allow for grammatical aspect marking (p. 71–72)
   a. *debe* 'owe'
   b. *gusta* 'like'
   c. *kosta* 'cost'
   d. *bal* 'be worth, cost'
   e. *stima* 'love'
   f. *meresé* 'deserve'
   g. *parse* 'seem, look like'
   h. *nifiká* 'mean'

He points out, regarding those in (16) that, "[t]he only way to mark these verbs explicitly for past time reference is with *tabata*." – the past Imperfective aspect marker (p. 71). In this group in (16) he makes special reference to *konosé* 'know (someone)' which can be used with the Imperfective aspect marker *a*. In such a case, he points out that "it then loses its stative meaning, and means entry into a state"- the equivalent of the English verb *met*." (p. 93, fn 6). We see here again sensitivity to inherent aspect and the interaction between this and grammatical aspect. The case of the difference in meaning which results when *konosé*

2.2 Some contributions to the study of Aspect in CECs

'know (someone)' appears with the Imperfective aspect marker reinforces my position that rather than focusing on a clear restriction between Imperfective aspect marking and Stative verbs, the interest should be in the interpretation that arises.

Andersen's indication that there may be at least two groups of Stative verbs is consistent with my observations for CECs. In Chapters 4 and 5, I point to three subgroups within the group of property items in CECs which may be labeled Stative: Those that do not allow for Non-stative expression and are thus incompatible with Progressive aspect and do not appear in transitive use; those which allow for Non-stative use and express a Change of state; and those which in Non-stative use express a Process. The suggestion based on the observation of the behaviour of such items is that the Class of Stative verbs may be as complex as that of Non-stative verbs.

2.2.8 Sidnell (2002)

This work merits some mention here as it directly contributes to the body of work in CECs with a direct focus on Aspect. Sidnell's focus is grammatical aspect in GC and in particular the expression of Habitual and Imperfective marking in GC. In looking at this area he points to the relevance of inherent aspect to grammatical aspect marking, stating that the "[c]hoice of preverbal marker is shown to be strongly conditioned by the stativity of the predicate (in the case of habituals)" (p. 151). In contrast to Bickerton (1975) Sidnell observes that

> [t]he co-occurrence of Imperfective *a* with stative predicates is in fact rather well attested in CGC[21] ... and in general there is nothing particularly odd about the marking of statives with *a*. (p. 166)

This observation of Sidnell, post Bickerton's citing of a restriction on this kind of occurrence, concurs with the position of Jaganauth (1987) and is more observationally adequate based on data that we have seen. Crucially, it brings us to a level where our interest is not just in the fact of such a co-occurrence but rather the interpretation of it.

In this regard, Sidnell examines data such as (18–19) which shows preverbal (d)*a* occurring with both Stative and Non-stative predicates:

(18) Sidnell (2002: 165)

    a. Dem **a** gat aal mi kotlas de.
        3PL ASP have all 1SG cutlass LOC
        'they always have all my cutlasses there.' (Habitual)

---

[21]Conservative Guyanese Creole, also Rural Guyanese Creole.

b. Sidnell (2002: 154)
   Di man dem a   de moor in sosaiiti. (Habitual)
   ART man PL   ASP COP more in society
   'The men tend to be more in the public spheres.'

(19) Sidnell (2002: 154)

   a. Shi a   pik plom, wen mi aks shi yestodee. (Progressive)
      3SG ASP pick plum when 1SG ask 3SG yesterday.
      'She was picking plums when I asked her yesterday.'
   b. Dem a   kot pikni soo? (Habitual)
      3PL ASP cut child so
      'Do they do autopsies on such small children?'
   c. Hiir, Linda a   kaal yu. (Progressive)
      hear Linda ASP call 2SG
      'Hear, Linda is calling you.'

We note here a variation between Habitual and Progressive in the aspectual interpretation of the marker *a* as it interacts with different predicates. In observing examples of this type Sidnell concludes that

> there do seem to be highly predictable constraints on the combination [i.e.: *a* + stative]. The use of *a* with stative predicates almost categorically results in habitual meaning[22] [...] Thus the interpretation of *a* with stative predicates is considerably more narrow than it is with non-statives where it expresses either progressive or habitual meaning. (p. 166)

This observation is supported by the fact that as we observe in the data above, the interpretation associated with the Stative predicates in (18) is strictly Habitual in comparison to the interpretation of Non-statives, which may be either Habitual or Progressive. Based on the different interpretations that may be associated with Non-stative predicates, however, Sidnell suggests that the Stative/Non-stative distinction may not be sufficient to account for what we see in Tense and Aspect marking and interpretation in CECs (p. 166).

In this regard, he points to a sub-categorization of both Stative and Non-stative predicates. Within the class of Non-statives, he points to verbs of motion (*gu*

---

[22] I suggest that the meaning may be even narrower with Statives; the meaning is more generic than it is Habitual since no iteration is indicated as is the case with Non-statives.

2.2 Some contributions to the study of Aspect in CECs

'go' *kom* 'come'), inceptives (*staat* 'start'), and a residual class including verbs of speaking (*taak* 'talk') and activity verbs (*waak* 'walk') (p. 166). Among Statives he also points to a complex group comprising modals (*kyan* 'can'), locatives (*de* 'be'), predicate adjectives (*nais* 'nice'), finite copula (*bii* 'be') and other Stative verbs (*ga/ge* 'get' (possessive), *noo* 'know'). This kind of sub-categorisation of both Statives and Non-Statives provides further insights into the notion of (Non-)Stativity and is at least in part consistent with my observation in §4.4 that there are additional concepts including MOTION, CONTACT etc. that further help to define the basic concept of Change.[23] Additionally, with regards to his observation of a complex group of Stative verbs, his observation supports my treatment of "dual aspectual forms" as characterised by a unique aspectual structure among property items.

Another point of interest raised by this work is the variation in the Stativity of a verb (predicate) based on its use. Like Jaganauth, Sidnell points to the verb *get* 'have' in CGC to illustrate variation in stativity:

(20) Variation in stativity of *get* according to use (Sidnell 2002: 167)
   a. Wan wan taim doz **get** mi ignorant.
      one one time does get 1SG ignorant
      'Once in a while (they) make me abusive.'
   b. Di children dem a **get** nalej.
      ART children PL ASP get knowledge
      'The children get the knowledge.'
   c. Mii aloon doz **get** a lak-op de.
      1SG alone does get a lock-up there
      'I am the only one who has a room which is often locked.'

Regarding these, Sidnell points out that in the case of (20a) and (20b), these instantiations of *get* in (20a–b) are Non-stative "roughly equivalent to "make" and "acquire"", respectively (p. 167). In (20c) however "the verb is equivalent to the English possessive "have" and is stative" (p. 167). Based on this, Sidnell points out that:

> [i]t is thus necessary to categorize many verbs according to their uses rather than according to some abstract lexical specification (which is perhaps what

---

[23]These notions are evident in the transitivity alternations (Levin 1993). However as I point out in Chapter 4, while they indicate different types of Change, they do not show an opposition between [+Change] and [−Change] which is the interest of this work.

Bickerton was trying to get at when he said that stativity applied to sentences rather than the verbs themselves. (p. 167)

What I suggest here is that what Sidnell calls the abstract representation of a verb and its actual use are related, since what we see here are different meanings associated with two homophonous and clearly related lexical items. As I pointed out previously, in the discussion of Jaganauth's data, these are semantically distinct items (although represented by identical forms). A speaker of the language would thus select one or the other based on the meaning that is intended. In other words, in my treatment, Sidnell's "abstract lexical specification" is not distinct from a verb's use. This is made clear in my discussion of Event Structures and primitives of Change in Chapters 4 and 5.

Nevertheless, what we encounter in Sidnell's work is a picture of Aspect in CECs that is more complex than many that we have seen so far in the field. This points to a need to further understand the semantics associated with particular predicates in order to account for the variation that we see in Aspect expression. This is consistent with my own findings; however, the question is at what level is this relevant? I maintain that the Stative/Non-stative distinction is relevant at the syntactic level as it relates to Telicity and even grammatical aspect marking. However, it is important to have an understanding of the lexico-semantic domain in order to account for semantic and syntactic differences that may arise in the interpretation of particular items. This is particularly relevant in the case of lexically identical forms associated with different meanings and forms expressing seemingly dual aspectual behaviours, which I treat in this work.

2.2.9 Gooden (2008)

Gooden's focus is Tense but it is worthy of mention here as it renews a call for attention to be paid to Aspect as a basic factor in understanding Tense.[24] Gooden argues that:

an analysis of both the aktionsarten of the verbs and discourse factors are critical to developing an understanding of the range of meanings and functions of both the relative past marker and the unmarked verb (p. 306)

Here we notice that she speaks from the perspective of Tense and points to the need for an understanding of inherent aspect in order to deal with Tense

---

[24]Cf. Alleyne (1980) for the suggestion that Aspect was perhaps more basic than Tense in the Creole Tense-Aspect system.

2.2 Some contributions to the study of Aspect in CECs

interpretation. Regarding Aspect, she points out that while there have been several analyses of Tense-Aspect in CECs "with some discussion of the influence of narrative structure [...] discussed comparatively less is the influence of lexical aspect [...] on Creole verbal morphology, though there are numerous discussions on the influence of stative and non-stative predicates." (p. 307). This suggests a distinction between *lexical aspect* and the Stative/Non-stative distinction indicating that in contrast to the approach of this work, Gooden does not apply this distinction at the lexical level.

Regarding "lexical aspect", however, she proposes that:

> a more fine-grained analysis of lexical aspect is needed, since an analysis simply in terms of the stative/non-stative distinctions does not account for all the facts. (p. 307)

This, as we see here is similar to Sidnell's observations and my perspective that further understanding of the lexico-semantic domain is necessary for a clearer understanding of Aspect.

Gooden's application of the Stative/Non-stative distinction is unlike that of Winford (1993) and Sidnell (2002) in that these notions are not applied to the verb but rather to the entire predicate or proposition. In Gooden's approach, Stativity is treated as a "feature of the lexical aspect (aktionsart) of the verb" (p. 315). However, although she refers to Aktionsart and lexical aspect, these terms do not apply at all to the verb for her. According to her:

> [s]ince aktionsart is a set of properties of predicates, i.e., verbs together with their objects and adjuncts, not just bare verbs, we must also examine the properties residing in the situation as a whole, not relying on identification on the basis of lexical form only. (p. 315–316)

As indicated here, Gooden does not refer to inherent aspect in the sense of that which is contained in the verb but rather the entire predicate including adjuncts. This approach takes Aspect to be compositional. consistent with the approach articulated in this work. However, her focus is on the whole rather than on parts comprising the whole. With this approach we are still left with the question of the precise contribution of the various elements, including the verb itself.

Gooden follows authors such as Dowty (1979) in applying several classes of situation types to events (Accomplishment, Achievement, Activity, State etc.) and applies the features Static, Durative Telic to these. The result is that although the discussion is seemingly about "lexical aspect" (suggesting the verb) this does not apply to the verb at all in any direct way but rather the entire predicate. The examples below are provided to illustrate her distinctions:

(21) Gooden (2008: 316)

    a. Mary baked the turkey in five hours. (accomplishment)

    b. Mary won the race. (achievement)

    c. Mary drove the car. (activity)

    d. Mary loves John. (state)

    e. Mary coughed. (semelfactive)

As shown here, the distinctions employed are applied to the entire predicate. Thus we are still left with the question regarding the unique contribution of the verb. This issue is discussed in my first chapter where I address issues associated with terminology and the need for a model which, though compositional, takes into account the unique contribution of the different but related elements in the composition of Aspect.

In contrast to her application of the Stative/Non-stative distinction to the entire predicate, Gooden's tests for Stativity appear to apply to verbs themselves. Speaking of the possible differences in lexical aspect between (morphologically) similar English and Belizean Creole (BC) verbs she points out that:

> Although the bulk of BC verbs are derived from English, there is no reason to expect their lexical aspects to be identical and indeed they are not. (p. 316).

As indicated here she seems to be talking about the verbs themselves and the relevant tests are applied to the verbs in question. Essentially in her test for Stativity, a verb is deemed Non-stative if it occurs under the following conditions:

(22) Gooden's (p. 317) tests for Non-stativity

    a. in the progressive

    b. as complements of non-volitional verbs e.g.: *force, persuade*

    c. with certain adverbials, e.g.: *deliberately, carefully* (etc.);

    d. permit verb-phrase anaphoric forms e.g. *do so* (Mufwene 1984)

Based on these tests she points out that verbs such as *biliiv* 'believe', *tink* 'think', *nuo* 'know' in BC "are rendered as stative since they do not occur in the specified contexts." (p. 318).

2.2 Some contributions to the study of Aspect in CECs

Gooden raises some important issues in the discussion of Aspect and recognises the complexity of Aspect outside of just grammatical marking. Her main contribution includes a call to pay more attention to lexical aspect and the fact that this may be more than the Stative/Non-stative distinction. I join with her in the call for a more in depth study of the lexical aspect of the verb. However, where for Gooden lexical aspect is not purely the verb but includes information that may be contained in the predicate, I aim to identify the specific semantic contribution of the verb to Aspect.

2.2.10 Youssef (2003)

This work successfully pinpoints one main issue that has mitigated against the overall effectiveness of Tense-Aspect studies in CECs. The main issue it deals with is terminology. This is significant as while authors have pointed to this as an issue (Winford 1993; 2001), we have not seen a work dedicated to addressing this for consistencies in general works in the field and directly calling for the use of "a consensual use of labels." (p. 81). In this regard, Youssef notes that:

> It is necessary for writers in Creole linguistics to make specific recourse to the work of language typologists when using the terminology of the field; otherwise they run the risk of using terms in narrow and particular ways which obscure the field rather than clarify it. (p. 81)

Similarly Winford (1993; 1997; 2001) observes that it is perhaps due to this that we have not been able to significantly impact the general field of linguistics. In discussing terminological issues, Youssef explores works such as that of Bickerton (1975), Holm (1988), Solomon (1993) and Winford (1993) where she notes differences in the analysis of the null grammatical aspect marker and aspectual *done* and the references to its function. Table 2.3 is a summary of her observations.

We see here varied analyses for both the null marker and aspectual *done* by the different authors. As previously indicated, for Bickerton (1975), the null marker is analysed from the perspective of Tense where it indicates either Past or Non-past depending on the Stativity of the verb. Youssef points out that for Holm (1988), the null marker indicates focus time (from a discourse perspective). Solomon (1993) and Winford (1993) provide an analysis from the perspective of Aspect but these also differ. Youssef separates Solomon (1993) from the other authors by pointing out that he "makes the clearest case so far for NULL as marking perfectivity in Creoles regardless of inherent meaning." (p. 92). According to him:

2 Aspect in Caribbean English Creoles: An overview of works

A "state" is nothing but the result of an "action", that is a completed "action". One is dead because one has died; one is married because one has got married; one loves because the process of falling in love is complete. We can group all the unmarked predicators as having the meaning 'completed' or perfective. (Solomon 1993: 96 as cited in Youssef 2003: 92)

Table 2.3: Interpretations associated with the null marker and *done* in CECs. (Youssef 2003: 96)

	Bickerton	Holm	Solomon	Winford 1993; 2000
NULL	Past/non-past	Focus time	Perfective Completive Completion Relevance	Perfective Perfect (1993) Unmarked (2000)
Done	Completive Resultative Perfect	Completive/Perfect	Perfective Completive Completion Relevance	Completion Resultative (1993) Completive Perfect (2000)

Solomon seems to be in line with both Voorhoeve (1957) and Alleyne (1980) who considered bare verbs representing Completive and Perfective respectively with no reference to inherent Aspect. Apparently, for Solomon, the Perfective/Non-perfective captures completion in an event so "Perfective means that the event expressed by the predicator is to be regarded as completed: non-perfective means that it is not to be so regarded." (Solomon 1993: 96 in Youssef 2003: 91). However, based on Solomon's approach it seems that Aspect would be based almost solely on grammatical aspect and not much else.

Winford (1993), as indicated in §2.2.6, analyses the null marker as a marker of Perfectivity. However, for him; Perfectivity is not necessarily associated with completion as it is made to cover Habituals and Generics as well. Youssef comments on this suggesting that there could "in fact [be] two NULLS in the system described, one perfective and the other Imperfective" (p. 93). She argued for these in the context of the Creole continuum and the "neutrality" established by unmarkedness. This, she argues, could allow for the form to have "markedly different functions in different parts of the system." (Youssef 1995 as cited in Youssef 2003: 93.) This brings into focus the difference between form and meaning. As we have seen before, the same form can have different functions depending on its

2.2 Some contributions to the study of Aspect in CECs

appearance and use in terms of context. In this sense, as Winford (1993) indicates, a form has both a primary (default) and a secondary meaning and function.

Youssef adjusts her view that perhaps there are two nulls in the system by reflecting

> [m]ore recently, however, I have recognized the potential for an overall compatibility in the broad categorical labelling applied: It ultimately becomes clear that virtually any kind of time span can be viewed either Perfectively or Imperfectively. (p. 93).

This later perspective captures what is the essence of grammatical marking as it is meant to provide a viewpoint of a situation and does not necessarily concern itself with the nature of the situation. Thus, the situation may be completed or not, Habitual or only once, and the speaker can choose a viewpoint not restricted by the nature of the situation.

As far as aspectual *done* is concerned Youssef points to a level of consensus: All authors seem to associate this in some way with the meaning Completive, while at least three of the four under review associate this with the Perfect (Bickerton, Holm and Winford). Solomon, like Alleyne (1980) sees *done* as a reinforcer of Perfective meaning. As we can see from this, ascribing a particular meaning to a marker is not necessarily an easy matter, in fact it appears to be quite difficult especially given the fact that discourse does affect the meaning that may arise from the use of a particular form. In this regard, Youssef points out that

> In ascribing tense to NULL, we recognise that writers are generally reacting to context and the inherent meaning of verbs rather than merely grammaticalized meaning; (p. 96)

She also points out that

> It is clear that *use* is a particular issue in distinguishing among forms which otherwise appear to share the same *meanings*. We need to specify the detail of contextual use of forms more precisely when we are specifying the functions of the markers we are describing. (p. 97)

As indicated here, there are a number of elements that we need to take into account in ascribing meaning to grammatical aspect markers. It seems that for many authors, interpretation of a particular marker may differ according to the type of verb with which it interacts and, as Youssef points out here as well, the context. Based on what we have seen so far, however, and in particular in the work of Sidnell (2002), the different interpretations that may be associated with a form are predictable. In other words, it may not be necessary to associate a particular grammatical form with all the meanings that may be indicated through its use. A more fruitful approach may be to indicate the base or default function or meaning of such a form. In these regards, Youssef points out that

> It is essential then that in every analysis we specify the exact way in which we are defining the use of these terms as well as considering how they have been used by other writers we discuss. The more abstract conceptualization of the categories perfective, imperfective and perfect are ultimately most useful in providing a consistent overall categorization schema (p. 102)

This is in line with the approach which I have taken in this work. As explained in Chapter 1, terminology within Aspect has to be defined based on the different levels and elements involved in aspectuality. From this perspective, meanings arising from the interaction between different areas of Aspect may not be associated with the unique contribution of a particular element. Thus, for example an Imperfective aspect marker may be interpreted as Habitual or Progressive in particular contexts, but this is not necessarily the meaning of the marker itself but rather an instantiation of different types of Imperfective meanings due to the interaction between factors such as the form itself, other elements in the utterance and also context.

Youssef's main contribution to the discussion of Tense-Aspect may be seen as a call to pay attention to and address the issues associated with terminology in field. This marks a step towards consolidating the different contributions that have been made so far in the discussion and also pointing us in the direction where our studies can be merged with more general studies in the field of general linguistics theory.

In §2.3, I will summarise the major issues arising out of the studies that have been discussed above.

2.3 Observations

One crucial issue that comes out of the discussion of works concerns the notion of Stativity and how this affects Tense-Aspect interpretation in Creole languages. While earlier writers such as Voorhoeve (1957) and later Alleyne (1980) may be said to avoid any overt reference to this notion, later authors starting with Bickerton (1975) address this as an area of importance and concern in Creole studies. Issues associated with the concept of Stativity stem from its application as evidenced in the works of not only Bickerton (1975) but also Jaganauth (1987), Gooden (2008) and Sidnell (2002). In the case of Bickerton (1975) we see that although his discussion points to a classification of verbs, he indicates that the distinction must apply to propositions rather than to verbs in order to account for the case of forms which are identical but display different uses consistent with expressions of Stativity and Non-stativity.

Faced with data signaling the same phenomenon, Jaganauth uncompromisingly rejects the relevance of the Stative/Non-stative distinction. Gooden (2008) points to a treatment at the level of the entire sentence but her tests for Stativity target the verbs themselves. Sidnell (2002) is very perceptive in his suggestion that the groups of Statives and Non-statives are complex and defined based on additional concepts which account for their interpretations. However, his overall treatment does not allow him to make a connection between lexical specification and the semantic use of forms in dealing with seemingly dual aspectual forms. In this regard, he, like Bickerton points to a classification of forms according to their uses rather than abstract lexical specification. Although authors such as Winford accept the Stative/Non-stative distinction as applied to the verb, without an addressing items which appear in both Stative and Non-stative use as exemplified in Jaganauth's examples above, the concept of verbs classified as Stative or Non-stative remains a mere intuition rather than an applied and explained concept.

In the chapters which follow, I will first present the specific case of property items and the problem presented by these as it relates to the Stative/Non-stative distinction (Chapter 3). In Chapter 4, I will elaborate the Stative/Non-stative distinction and the feature Change and will present a categorisation for this general group of items in Chapter 5.

3 The problem of dual aspectual forms

3.1 Introduction

In this chapter, I will outline how authors have attempted to address what they evaluate as the problem presented by some property items, namely those which appear in multiple uses and specifically those that I refer to as DUAL ASPECTUAL FORMS.[1] Typical items as *ded, weeri, sik*, etc., may be used to express the Stative meanings 'dead' 'be tired', and 'be sick' respectively as well as the Non-stative meanings 'die', 'become/make tired' and 'become/make sick'. As indicated previously (Chapter 1) the two issues that have been addressed regarding this group of items are:

1. Their categorial status as either verbs or adjectives

2. Their aspectual status in relation to the Stative/Non-stative distinction

In this work, both issues will be treated as logically related to each other, with the issue of the aspectual status of these items being primary in relation to the question of categorial status. From this perspective, the determination of the aspectual status of a lexical item in this group as either Stative or Non-stative is logically tied to a status as adjective or verb respectively. Thus there is basically one major question to be answered and the other follows as a consequence. This however is not necessarily the way in which these items have been treated in the literature.[2] Thus, I will outline the treatment of these as two issues in the sections which follow.

In §3.2 I will evaluate the way in which various authors have attempted to deal with the issue of the categorial status of this group of items. The discussion will focus, first, on the debate between authors Sebba (1986) and Seuren (1986),

---

[1] Recall that my use of the term "dual aspectuality" is intended to capture the fact that these items appear in both Stative and Non-stative use.

[2] Note for example that while Kouwenberg (1996) assumes adjectival status for the Stative use, and verbal status for Non-stative use, in the case of Winford (1993), there is a division on the basis of Stativity but he assumes a group consisting solely of verbs.

3 The problem of dual aspectual forms

who take seemingly opposed positions on the matter: Sebba adopts the "standard" view that these items are (Stative) verbs; Seuren adopts the view that they are adjectives introduced by a null copula. We will see that neither of these viewpoints can deal satisfactorily with the diversity that is presented in the data, and that a more differentiated approach is called for. Finally, I will consider the arguments put forward by Kouwenberg (1996), who analyses this group of items as containing both verbs and adjectives.

In §3.3, I will look at the question of the aspectual status of dual aspectual forms and the Stative/Non-stative distinction. This question of the aspectual status of these items is less overtly discussed than that of their categorial status, but Winford (1993) represents the most complete attempt to address this group of items from this perspective. His treatment will be outlined in §3.4 and evaluated based on some JC data. An examination of Winford's proposal will point to the desirability of an alternative model which categorises items based on their aspectual behaviour as determined through a combination of syntactic and semantic criteria, rather than the semantic notions of Dixon (1977) which Winford draws on. Such a model will be presented in Chapter 5. I will return to the issue of categorial status in Chapter 6.

3.2 Verb or adjective? The categorial status of property items

3.2.1 The Sranan case: A debate between Sebba and Seuren

As indicated in Chapter 2, the standard analysis for property items in CECs since Voorhoeve (1957) is that these items in predicative use are essentially (Stative) verbs (cf. Alleyne 1980; Jaganauth 1987; etc). This is the view adopted by Sebba (1986). Nonetheless, based on data from Sranan (SR), Sebba (1986) argues that a form such as *bradi* 'broad' has dual categorial status appearing as both an adjective (1a) and a (Stative) verb (1b). This classification is based on its syntactic appearance with or without the locative/existential copula *de* and modifying material such as 'so'. Compare:

(1) SR (adapted from Sebba 1986: 112)

    a. A   liba   de   [so **bradi**].
        art river cop   so broad
        'The river is so broad.'

3.2 Verb or adjective? The categorical status of property items

    b. A liba [**bradi** so].
       art river [broad so]
       'The river is so broad.'

Thus, in (1a) *bradi* satisfies the syntactic condition of an adjective by appearing with the copula *de* while it is said to be a Stative verb where it appears without the copula in (1b). I will return to the significance of (1a) below. Based on the predicative use of an item such as *bradi* in (1b), Sebba (1986) argues that

> while there is a separate category "adjective" in Sranan , the class of objects which corresponds to "predicate adjective" in English must be regarded as verbs in Sranan. (p. 110)

It is worth noting that Sebba seems to address here the entire class of predicates labeled "predicate adjectives" in English. This would essentially coincide with the class of property items that I discuss below in §3.4 (see Table 3.1, "Property concepts in CECs"). As we will see there, these constitute a diverse group of items based not only on their semantic denotations but also on their syntactic behaviour. Sebba's arguments for predicative property items as Stative verbs, however, are based on differences and similarities that he observes between what he labels as attributive adjectives, predicative adjectives and Stative verbs.

Sebba treats adjectives as a subclass of Stative verbs based on what he considers to be the "well-known semantic similarity between verbs and predicate adjectives" and the "obvious similarity in the syntactic behavior of Sranan stative verbs like *lobi* 'like, love' and predicate adjectives like *tranga* 'strong'" (p. 114). The examples in (2–5) below show their distributional similarity (all adapted from Sebba 1986: 114):

(2)   a. Rudy **lobi** dagu so.
         Rudy love dog so
         'Rudy so likes dogs.'

      b. Rudy **tranga** so.
         Rudy strong so
         'Rudy is so strong.'

(3)   a. Rudy ben **lobi** dagu.
         Rudy TNS love dog
         'Rudy loved dogs.'

3 The problem of dual aspectual forms

    b. Rudy ben **tranga** so.
       Rudy TNS strong so
       'Rudy was so strong.'

(4) a. Rudy e   **lobi** dagu.
         Rudy ASP love dog
         'Rudy is starting to like dogs.'

    b. Rudy e   **tranga**.
         Rudy ASP strong
         'Rudy is getting strong.'

As these examples indicate, the distribution of a form such as *tranga* 'strong' as it relates to Tense-Aspect markers appears to be identical to that of a Stative verb such as *lobi* 'like, love'. Moreover, (5) shows that neither *tranga* nor *lobi* is acceptable after a copula:

(5) a. * Rudy de **lobi** dagu
         Rudy COP love dog

    b. * Rudy de **tranga**
         Rudy COP strong

Recall (1a), which seemed to show that it is possible for a predicative adjective to be introduced by a copula. Sebba points out that it is the presence of *so* or other types of quantifying elements which makes this possible; he calls the phrases that are thus formed "Extent Phrases" and claims that these provide a context for the predicative use of adjectives.

Sebba's analysis centers as well on the obvious differences in the distribution of attributive and predicative adjectives. In this regard he notes that

> attributive adjectives precede the nominal they modify; any quantifiers, etc. which modify them occur before the adjectives. This is in contrast to the behaviour of modifiers with *predicate* adjectives which in most cases *follow* the adjective. (p. 114–115)

This is based on observation of data such as that shown below in (6) and (7):

(6) Attributive adjectives (Sebba 1986: 115)

    a. wan **bigi** dagu
        a   big dog

3.2 Verb or adjective? The categorial status of property items

b. $\left\{\begin{array}{ll} \text{(wan)} & \text{(tumsi)} \\ \text{a} & \text{too} \\ \\ \text{(someni)} & \text{(moro)} \\ \text{so.many} & \text{more} \end{array}\right\}$ **bigi** dagi
   big dog

(7) Predicative adjectives (Sebba 1986: 115)

    a. A   dagu bigi tumsi.
       the dog big too.much/very
       'The dog is too big.'

    b. A   dagu moro bigi
       the dog more big
       $\Big\}$ leki trawan.
    c. A   dagu bigi moro
       the dog big more
       than the.other.one
    'The dog is bigger than the other one.'

This difference in the distribution of predicative and attributive adjectives, leads Sebba to conclude that, "in Sranan, attributive adjectives must be treated as a class distinct from both verbs and predicate adjectives." (p. 115). According to him,

> there is reason to recognize an independent category Adjective […] in Sranan, but […] predicate adjectives are in fact members of the category V (verb) and behave like stative verbs. (p. 116)

Seuren (1986) provides a different analysis of predicative adjectives, which he treats as adjectives in Sranan regardless of their syntactic realizations. Using the similar case of the presence or absence of the copula *de,* with such items as a part of his evaluation, (cf. 1 above) he acknowledges the existence of cases where the presence of *de* signals a difference in meaning as in (8) below:

(8) a. A   **bun**.
     3SG good
     'That/he is ok.'

   b. A   **de bun**.
     3SG COP good
     'He is doing alright.'

3 The problem of dual aspectual forms

The semantic difference signaled here based on the translation provided, is one between an individual and stage level interpretation, (8a) and (8b) respectively. However, according to Seuren, variations in meanings due to the presence of *de* are "few in number and not of a general nature " (p. 124). More frequent it seems are "regular and predictable alternations" such as those in (9) and (10) below:

(9) Sranan (adapted from Seuren 1986: 124)

    a. Mi futu no **bigi so**.
       1SG foot NEG big so
       'My foot is not so big.'

    b. Mi futu no de so **bigi**.
       1SG foot NEG COP so big
       'My foot is not so big.'

(10) Sranan (adapted from Seuren 1986: 124)

    a. A liba **bradi**.
       ART river broad
       'The river is wide.'

    b. O **bradi** a liba **bradi**?
       how broad ART river broad
       'How wide is the river?'

    c. O **bradi** a liba de?
       how broad ART river COP
       'How wide is the river?'

    d. A liba musu **bradi**.
       ART river must broad
       'The river must be wide.'

    e. A liba musu de **bradi**.
       ART river must COP broad
       'The river must be wide.'

As noted here, the copula *de* with an item such as *bradi* varies in its syntactic appearance without any notable change in meaning. Based on data such as this, Seuren posits that the presence or absence of *de* is predictably linked to the existence of an underlying copula BE. According to him, this BE copula,

3.2 Verb or adjective? The categorial status of property items

manifests itself as a zero morpheme (ø) when it finds itself in the position of a finite verb form and is followed directly by an adjective, but as *na* or *de* otherwise, in the same position. When BE is infinitival, the use of *de* is optional when it is directly followed by an adjective; otherwise it is obligatory. (p. 124)

This observation essentially allows him to treat the various occurrences of items such as *bigi* 'big' and *bradi* 'broad' simply as adjectives where Sebba posits a difference in categorial status in the different instantiations.

From Seuren's perspective the standard analysis of predicative adjectives as (Stative) verbs "seems to have a lot going for it, since on superficial inspection, adjectives seem to behave like verbs". However, he points out that the "parallelism breaks down when the facts are inspected more closely" (p. 123). In particular, he highlights a difference between Stative verbs and adjectives whereby "adjectives but not stative verbs, allow for *causative* uses as well" (p. 127). For example, an item such as *tranga* 'strong' may be used as a causative while the same is not possible for a verb like *lobi* 'love'. Compare:

(11)   Sranan (Seuren 1986: 127)

   a.   Alen e   tranga yu.
        rain ASP strong you
        'Rain makes you strong.'

   b. * Sopi e   lobi yu a   uma   dati.
        booze makes you love the woman that
        'Booze makes you love that woman.'

As shown here (in 11), a causative variation is possible with an item such as *tranga* 'strong' but not with a regular Stative verb like *lobi* 'love'. This and other differences in the distributional properties of *tranga* and *lobi* show, according to Seuren, "that there *is* a difference between predicate adjectives and stative verbs" (Seuren 1986: 127).

A general objection to both Sebba's and Seuren's positions is that neither is able to deal with variation in the class of items they consider. It is interesting for me that both Sebba and Seuren use individual items, such as *bradi* 'broad' or *tranga* 'strong' to represent the distribution of predicative property items in Sranan. A question that logically arises here for me, is whether or not the distribution of an adjective such as *tranga* 'strong' is the same as that of, for instance, *bigi* 'big' or *bradi* 'broad'. Below, in §3.4, we will see that property items are varied in their behaviour. This means that the conclusion drawn by Sebba of a clear

3 The problem of dual aspectual forms

similarity in the distribution of predicate adjectives and Stative verbs on the basis of the behaviour of a single item is invalidated. At best, it may only be applicable to a particular class of predicative property items rather than to this class in general. Similarly, not every property item is able to participate in the causative variation which Seuren points to as a property which distinguishes these items from stative verbs. In short, an analysis which generalises over the behaviour of predicative adjectives must consider more closely the behaviour of the range of property items rather than just a few individual items.[3]

This point can be illustrated by considering the variation in transitivity (and Stativity) that items such as *tranga* 'strong/make strong' display (see example 11a), or even the simple fact that every one of these items is at least *some* times an adjective. Both Seuren and Sebba attempt to account for the syntactic appearance of the property items: Sebba, by positing two categories for these items based on their syntactic realisation (attributive vs. predicative) and Seuren by positing something of an abstract generative device that predicts the different appearances, linking these to one category (adjective). But neither of these treatments accounts for the fact that these items are able to behave the way they do in the first place – an issue which I will attempt to address in Chapters 4 and 5.

In §5.3, I will posit for cases similar to *tranga* 'strong/make strong' that Nonstative elements of meaning such as CAUSE or BECOME are present or may be introduced in the Event Structure of such items allowing for this variation. It is the presence of these at the lexico-semantic level that distinguishes inherently dual aspectual forms (Transitions) from regular Stative verbs which have an Event Structure of State. This means that predicate adjectives of the type indicated by *tranga* 'strong' are indeed semantically distinct from Stative verbs; however, they are also distinct from other predicate adjectives which do not allow for this causative variation[4] – a possibility not considered by Seuren.

---

[3]Another weakness in Sebba's argumentation can be seen in the fact that he, despite his view that predicative property items are Stative verbs, nonetheless needs these items to be distinct from Stative verbs on the basis of their multi-functionality. He points out that "all Sranan adjectives may also function as nominals which denote their abstract quality, e.g. *ogri*, Adj: 'ugly, bad' ; N: 'evil (deed)'; *fri* Adj.: 'free' N: 'freedom'. This possibility of multi-functionality applies across the board to Sranan adjectives but only to a subset of verbs. e.g., *singi* V: 'sing' N: 'song'. Thus while multifunctional verbs would either have to be listed as both V and N in the lexicon [...] the label adjective (A) would be sufficient to mark an item as also a member of the category N" (p. 116)

[4]While I do not deal with this issue here, indications are that there may be some kind of semantic feature associated with these items that sets them apart in the lexicon as vulnerable to the causative variation. Based on Winford (1993), this may be the strength of a feature akin to the notions TRANSITORY or PERMANENT whereby items which are most transitory would be those most likely to be affected. This of course would vary according to speech community accounting for the differences in the behaviour of similar items across CECs.

3.2 Verb or adjective? The categorial status of property items

In the section which follows, I will look at the analysis presented by Kouwenberg (1996) which may be said to be distinct from that of both Sebba (1986) and Seuren (1986) in its clear acknowledgement of the categorial diversity of this group of items.

3.2.2 Kouwenberg (1996)

A defining feature of Kouwenberg (1996) is her recognition of a diverse categorial status for the group of adjectival predicates[5] in Caribbean Creoles. According to her, "part of the problematic nature of the issue results from attempts to treat a large and diverse class of forms as a single class for which a unified account is sought" (p. 27). Thus, in contrast to other authors who argue for the status of adjectival predicates as either verbs or adjectives, Kouwenberg (1996) acknowledges a group of forms comprising both (Non-stative) verbs and adjectives. With reference to data from Saramaccan (SM), Sranan (SR) and Berbice Dutch Creole (BD), she argues for the existence of a class of adjectives which have related verbs. According to her:

> In view of the existence of a class of forms that may appear in the attributive position, as complements of copular verbs, in comparative constructions, and in – SR – in question phrases, the existence of a class of adjectives in the Creole languages under discussion is, I think, indisputable. That these languages also have verbs which are somehow related to these adjectives follows from facts such as the ability of these forms to appear as predicates with an imperfective marker, to participate in predicate cleft, and to take object NPs. (p. 32)

From this perspective, she does not argue either against a position that posits adjectivals as verbs or as adjectives but rather against the idea that these items fall into one single class.

In examples such as (12), she points out that the attributive elements *satu* 'salted' (SM), *bradi* 'broad' (SR) and *potɛ* 'old' (BD) are adjectives:

(12) a. Saramaccan
  di satu gwamba
  ART salt meat
  'the salted meat'

---

[5]Note that Kouwenberg utilises the term "adjectivals" in reference to this group of items.

3 The problem of dual aspectual forms

    b. Sranan
       a   bradi liba
       ART broad river
       'the wide river'

    c. Berbice Dutch
       di   potɛ jɛrma
       ART old woman
       'the old woman"

The behaviour of adjectivals in this position seems quite uniform and as Kouwenberg points out distinguishes them from "real verbs" which for the most part do not appear in such positions.[6] (p. 30).

Where such forms are similar to verbs in terms of their ability to appear with Imperfective aspect, Kouwenberg highlights a difference in the behaviour of some items as opposed to others. In this regard, she points out that "there is a class of BD adjectivals which pattern fully with action verbs such as *kain* 'pick' in that they appear quite unproblematically with aspectual suffixes" while there are those which "may appear in perfective forms but not in imperfective forms" (p. 30). This difference is highlighted in the behaviour of BD items such as *gu* 'big', which patterns with Non-stative verbs, as opposed to *potɛ* 'old', which does not show the same range of possibilities, as shown in (13):

(13) (Kouwenberg 1996: 30)

    a. Berbice Dutch (BD)
       Titi ju **gwarɛ**...
       time 2SG big.IPF
       'When you are growing up...'
       cf. ju krikja gu
          2SG get.IPF big
       'you are getting big/growing up.'

    b. Berbice Dutch
       Eni masi gugutɛ   nau.
       3PL must big.big.PF now
       'They must be big/have grown up by now.'
       cf. Eni gu.
          3PL big
       'They are big.' (inherent or acquired)

---

[6] Winford (1993) points to a small group of verbs in JC and GC which appear in attributive position.

3.2 Verb or adjective? The categorial status of property items

(14) Berbice Dutch

   a. (X) potɛtɛ na, timi kori ababaka.
      (X) old.PF now, able work anymore.NEG
      '(X) has got old, (he) cannot work anymore.'
      cf. O potɛ.
         3SG old
      'He is old.'

   b. * o pota
      cf. O krikja potɛ.
         3SG get.IPF old
      'She is getting old."

In these examples, Kouwenberg points out that while, *gu* 'big' can appear in both Perfective and Imperfective use, *potɛ* 'old' is more restrictive in that while it appears in Perfective use, "a process interpretation can be expressed only by use of a construction which contains a copular verb." (p. 30)

Due to the difference noted in the behaviour of *gu* 'big' on one hand and *potɛ* 'old' on the other, Kouwenberg assumes two classes of adjectivals. Essentially for her, *gu* 'big' "belongs simultaneously to the class of adjectives and the class of (intransitive process) verbs", while, *potɛ* 'old', "joins the class of verbs through a productive derivation which relates derived intransitive process verbs to base adjectives." (p. 36). In recognising two groups of adjectivals, Kouwenberg (1996) is most similar to Winford (1993) who also notes a split in this group of items based on their compatibility with Imperfective aspect. However, where Kouwenberg distinguishes two groups, comprising verbs and adjectives, Winford sees a group of verbs differentiated based on Stativity: one group is Stative while the other is Non-stative).

3.2.3 A note on later works

Winford (1997) and Migge (2000) are among later authors to weigh in on the discussion of the categorial status of these items. Similar to Kouwenberg (1996) these authors recognise a flexible categoriality associated with property items but align more closely with the analysis of these items as verbs as proffered by Sebba (1986). Specifically, both Winford (1997) and Migge (2000) uphold treatment of these items as verbs displaying flexible Stativity, but also make allowances for these items as "adjectives in certain functions" (Winford 1997: 249) when occurring as prenominal attributives. In treating these items, Winford (1997) calls on

3 The problem of dual aspectual forms

syntactic criteria such as their ability to appear with TMA markers and adverbial modifiers; their ability to undergo "predicate cleft" and their appearance in modifying serial verb constructions (p. 257). Migge (2000) reflects a similar analysis. Neither of these works contributes new arguments to the discussion on the categorial status of these items.

In the case of Winford, while he addresses the categorial status of these items, his treatment of their aspectual status as put forward in his (1993) work reflects, in my estimation, his principal contribution to this discussion and this is the view that underlies the analysis that we see in later works. In §3.4, I will examine Winford's (1993) analysis of property items from the perspective of aspectual status rather than categorial status. Here, I will first turn to the broader issue of Stativity as explored in the literature on Caribbean Creoles.

3.3 The question of the Stative/Non-stative distinction

As mentioned in Chapter 2, data such as (15–16) below which contain the property items *sik* 'sick', *weeri* 'weary' and *redi* 'ready' have been called upon to question the validity of the Stative/Non-stative distinction and the notion of a unique contribution of the verb to Aspect in CECs:

(15) Guyanese Creole (GC) Stative usage
 (Jaganauth 1987: 31)
 a. Mi **sik**.
  1SG sick
  'I am sick.'
 b. Mi **weeri**.
  1SG weary
  'I am weary.'
 c. Shi **redi**.
  3SG ready
  'She is ready."

(16) GC Stative verbs in Non-stative use
 (Jaganauth 1987: 31)
 a. Da tablit **sik** mi stomik.
  that tablet sick 1SG stomach
  'That pill has made me ill.'

3.3 The question of the Stative/Non-stative distinction

b. Dis baskit **weeri** mi.
   this basket weary 1SG
   'This basket has made me tired.'

c. I **redi** shi.
   3SG ready 3SG
   'He has gotten her ready.'

In these examples, the lexical items *sik* 'sick', *weeri* 'weary' and *redi* 'ready' appear in transitive constructions with Non-stative meanings (16) and also in intransitive constructions with Stative meanings (15).

Due to the existence of items such as these which appear in both Stative and Non-stative use, and also inconsistencies in Bickerton's observation of a clear difference in Tense interpretation of Stative as opposed to Non-stative verbs authors are divided on the validity of this distinction. On the one hand, there are authors like Winford (1993) who adopt a position that "certain predicators involve change or process while others do not" (p. 34). In addressing what he calls "apparent inconsistencies" in the behaviour of lexical items he explains that these "can be accounted for without abandoning the basic distinction between stative and non-stative verbal lexemes" (p. 29). Winford, explains variability in the behaviour of certain lexical items in the context of

> an ongoing process of decreolization, involving the apparent loss of transitivity in some cases and categorial shift from more verbal to a more truly adjectival status." (p. 196)

He posits that "[t]he most convenient solution would be for each item with a transitive function to be listed separately in the lexicon." (Winford 1993: 196). Without examining this position at this stage (see Chapters 5 and 6 for discussion), I am in agreement with Winford that the basic intuition associated with the Stative/Non-stative distinction need not be discarded. Rather, the different Tense-Aspect interpretations of Stative and Non-stative verbs point to a need to better understand this distinction and how it works. This is the viewpoint that is also implied by authors such as Andersen (1990) and Gooden (2008).

In contrast to Winford's position however, there are those authors who point to a conceptual flaw in Bickerton's (1975) claim of the Stative/Non-stative distinction as "crucial" in the Tense-Aspect system of creole languages. The issue essentially is, if it is the case that there are verbs that are Stative and those that are Non-stative, how does one account for lexical items that may be one or the other? Faced with the prospect of having listings in the lexicon of identical items

3 The problem of dual aspectual forms

differentiated only on the basis of Stativity, we may recall that authors such as Sidnell (2002) point to the actual use of a verb as determining the aspectual meaning it denotes rather than a lexical division of verbs. According to Sidnell (2002: 167) it is "necessary to categorize many verbs according to their uses rather than according to some abstract lexical specification[7]" (p. 167). By this he suggests a separation between the use of an item in context and the lexical specification of such a form; ultimately discarding the latter. This is the position of other authors in CECs such as Jaganauth (1987) who argues against a separation of verbs based on the Stative/Non-stative distinction due to the varying uses that they may display (see §2.2.5 for full discussion).

The problem with such approaches is that there is not a clear position on how Aspect as a cohesive system is to be treated in CECs. For example, items displaying the aspectual behaviour of those in (15) and (16) above form a class, but we do not see the same behaviour in all relevant forms in the language. Although these items fall within the larger class of property items, we will see below in §3.4 that not all items within this group display the same flexibility in behaviour: not all (Stative) property items allow for a contrasting Non-stative version or what I treat as the introduction of a causative or agentive element (Chapter 5). From this we see that there is a need to further understand this group of predicates and how they fit into a general system of Aspect. In other words, is there a mechanism that can account for the behaviour of such items while also accounting for the behaviour of clearly Stative and Non-stative items?

To date, not many authors have attempted to address the case of property items from the perspective of a holistic aspectual categorization. To my knowledge, Winford (1993) is unique in this respect as he addresses the entire group of property items rather than individual items of interest. In the following section, I will spend some time reviewing the analysis of Winford (1993). An evaluation of his classification will point to the desirability of a model which categorises items based on their aspectual behaviour (syntactic and semantic criteria) rather than the semantic notions of Dixon (1977) which form the basis of Winford's account.

---

[7] It is not clear what Sidnell means when he makes reference to "lexical specification". This could refer to the semantic categories of Dixon (1977) which Winford (1993) uses in his categorisation. If this is the case, then I do agree with him that this is not sufficient. However, in reference to the lexical template of an item, I will explore in Chapter 4 the notion of Event Structure and argue consistent with authors such as Pustejovsky (1991) and Levin (1993) that there is a part of the lexical specification of an item that "predicts the different uses that may be associated with a lexical item.

3.4 Winford's semantic categorisation of CEC property items and an evaluation

3.4.1 Winford's semantic categorisation of CEC property items

Table 3.1 shows Winford's categorisation of property items in CECs based on semantic concepts ranging from more temporary to more permanent (cf. Dixon 1977). As noted previously, Winford's analysis has been the only attempt at a generalisation over the behaviour of property items in CECs on the grounds of aspectual status.

As shown in Table 3.1, CEC property items may be classified based on semantic concepts ranging from those that are more temporary (i.e: Physical Property, Dimension and Colour) to those that are more permanent (Age, Value etc). Winford (1993) observes that the items most vulnerable to what I call dual aspectual interpretations are those denoting "transitory states" such as Physical Property, Dimension and Colour as opposed to those which represent more "permanent qualities" such as Age, Value, etc. (p. 184). Based on the ability of items to appear with Progressive Aspect marking and their ability to appear in transitive usage, he observes a general split in this semantic classification between items expressing Physical Property and all others (p. 187).

In his analysis, items which express Physical Property "behave rather like Change of state (process) verbs whose semantic features are compatible with Progressive aspect".[8] Hence, he labels them "essentially Non-stative" in comparison to items which express the semantic concepts of Dimension, Colour, Human Propensity which, according to him, "behave rather like Stative verbs" (p. 187–188). Thus, Winford's model predicts the aspectual status of CEC property items based on semantic concepts. His observation of a split in the Stativity of these items coincides with my own observation of some items being essentially Non-stative while others are Stative. However, the predictions which his model makes are not borne out, as I will show below. Moreover, I differ in my characterisation

---

[8]While I do not accept the compatibility of an item with Progressive aspect as a test for the Stativity of the form itself, the meaning that results where this interaction takes place provides insights into the inherent aspectual status of the items (see discussion in Chapter 5, §5.5). Thus for example with regular Non-stative verbs, we may note that the interpretation with the Progressive is generally that of an ongoing process with no Change of state implied while in the case of dual aspectual forms a Change of state interpretation comes into focus. (cf. examples in (18) below).

3 The problem of dual aspectual forms

Table 3.1: Property Concepts in CECs (adapted from Winford 1993: 184).

more transitory →→→→→→→→→→→→→→→→→→→→→→→→→→→→→→→→→→→→ more permanent

Physical property (A)	Dimension (B)	Colour (C)	Age (D)	Value (E)	Human propensity (F)	Speed (G)
ded 'dead'	big 'big'	blak 'black'	njuu 'new'	bad 'bad'	chupid 'stupid'	faas 'fast'
drai 'dry'	braad 'broad'	daak 'dark'	ool 'old'	gud 'good'	hapi 'happy'	kwik 'quick'
ful 'full'	fain 'fine'	griin 'green'	yong 'young'	nais 'nice'	jelas 'jealous'	sloo 'slow'
haad 'hard'	fat 'fat'	red 'red'			leezi 'lazy'	
hat 'hot'	lang 'long'	wait 'white'			mad 'mad'	
kool 'cold'	maaga 'slim'	yela 'yellow'			ruud 'rude'	
raip 'ripe'	shaat 'short'				wikid 'wicked'	
saaf 'soft'	smaal 'small'				wotlis 'worthless'	
sik 'sick'	taal 'tall'					
sowa 'sour'	waid 'wide'					
swiit 'sweet'						
wet 'wet'						

most vulnerable to dual aspectual interpretations →→→→→→→→→→→→→→→→→ least vulnerable to dual aspectual interpretations

inherently denote change of state | do not inherently denote change of state

72

3.4 Winford's semantic categorisation of CEC property items and an evaluation

of inherently Stative items as adjectives as opposed to Winford's characterisation of these items as (Stative) verbs (see Chapter 6 for discussion).

3.4.2 An evaluation

In this section I will evaluate Winford's model based on some JC data. Of interest here is whether or not items falling into a particular semantic category display the behaviour predicted. Recall that Winford cites a separation between property items of the semantic type Physical Property as Non-stative (i.e.: compatible with Progressive aspect) as opposed to items in other categories which are Stative. Here, I will attempt to highlight the basics of this separation based on some JC data. It will become evident that while there are items which fit the pattern that Winford suggests in terms of Stativity, there are also items which are inconsistent with the expected behaviour of their semantic group.

Starting with the group of items in category A (Physical Property), an item such as *ded* 'dead' in JC may be shown to be typical of this group in terms of its ability to express Non-stativity and in particular a Change of state. The way in which this interpretation is manifested varies as it may be contextually achieved (17a–b), expressed through the use of a temporal adverbial (17c) or evident in the use of Imperfective aspect marking (17d). Note that all JC data in this section (except where otherwise indicated) are drawn from my personal intuitions).

(17) Jamaican Creole (JC)

    a. Di man **ded**.
       ART man dead
        i. 'The man is dead.'
        ii. 'The man died.'

    b. Di man **ded** iina di aksident.
       ART man dead in the accident
       'The man died in the accident.'

    c. Di man **ded** sed spiid.
       ART man dead same speed
       'The man died immediately.'

    d. Di man a **ded**.
       ART man ASP dead
       'The man is dying.'

3 The problem of dual aspectual forms

The JC item *ded* 'dead' is shown here as ambiguous between a Stative and Non-stative interpretation in (17a) and clearly Non-stative in its interpretation in (17b–d). Winford labels items displaying the behaviour of *ded* 'dead' and falling into the category of items expressing Physical Property as Non-stative (Change of state).

Two questions arise from these observations. The first has to do with explanatory adequacy, and is the question of the labeling of an item which is able to express both Stativity and Non-stativity as "essentially non-stative", as Winford does (p. 184). This is an issue that I will deal with in Chapter 4 where I attempt to elucidate the notion of Change as associated with the Stative/Non-stative distinction and the conceptual question of how an item may be associated with both Stativity and Non-stativity. The second question has to do with observational adequacy given Winford's attempt at a generalisation over the behaviour of items based on their semantic class. Thus the question is whether or not all items falling into the group of Physical Property can be shown to display similar behaviours in terms of their ability to appear in Non-stative use. This is the question that I will deal with here.

Without paying attention to the specifics of how an item allows for the expression of Non-stativity[9], it is apparent that there are items in JC which, based on Winford (1993), fall into the semantic class of Physical Property but which are resistant to the expression of Non-stativity. Items such as *saaf* 'soft', *haad* 'hard', *swiit* 'sweet', *sowa* 'sour', etc., may be said to be a-typical of property items expressing Physical Property in that they do not appear to be compatible with Non-stative meaning. Compare:

(18) Jamaican Creole

    a. Di mango **saaf**.
        ART mango soft
        'The mango is soft.'

---

[9] In Chapter 5 I outline that Non-stativity may be indicated through the presence of Imperfective aspect marking, temporal adverbials and also in the case of the causative/inchoative alternation. However, there may be lexical items which show variation in their acceptance of all these contexts even where they allow for Non-stative expression. Thus, there may be an item which allows for transitive variation but does not allow for Imperfective aspect marking; in this way it allows for an interpretation that is Non-stative but resists Imperfective aspect marking. In this work, the focus is not on the range of Non-stative expression that is allowed but rather the fact that an item allows for such expression and the meaning that is indicated in such an instance.

3.4 Winford's semantic categorisation of CEC property items and an evaluation

    b. *Di mango a **saaf**.
        ART mango ASP soft
        'The mango is getting soft.'

    c. *Dem **saaf** di mango.
        3PL soft ART mango
        'They are softening/making the mango soft.'

(19) Jamaican Creole

    a. Di siment **haad**.
        ART cement hard
        'The cement is hard.'

    b. *Di siment a **haad**
        ART cement ASP hard
        'The cement is hardening.'

    c. *Dem **haad** di siment.
        3PL hard the cement
        'They made the cement hard.'

(20) Jamaican Creole

    a. Di lemanied **swiit**.
        ART lemonade sweet
        'The lemonade is sweet.'

    b. *Di lemanied a **swiit**.
        ART lemonade ASP sweet
        'The lemonade is getting sweet.'

    c. *Dem **swiit** di lemanied.
        3SG sweet the lemonade
        'They sweetened the lemonade/made the lemonade sweet.'

(21) Jamaican Creole

    a. Di juus **sowa**.
        ART juice sour
        'The juice is sour.'

    b. *Di juus a **sowa**.
        ART juice ASP sour
        'The juice is getting sour.'

3 The problem of dual aspectual forms

    c. * Dem pikni / laim **sowa** di   juus.
        PL   child / lime sour the juice
        'The children/limes made the juice sour.'

The examples (18–21) show the items *saaf* 'soft', *swiit* 'sweet', *sowa* 'sour' as resistant to Non-stative interpretations[10] in contrast to an item such as *ded* 'dead' which presumably falls in the same semantic category. This difference in aspectual behaviour suggests an aspectual split in the category of items semantically expressing Physical Property: while some are open to Non-stative expression, others are not.

In the case of items displaying the behaviour of *saaf* 'soft', *swiit* 'sweet', *sowa* 'sour', etc. these may be said to form a natural class with other items categorized as semantically expressing Age, Value, Human Propensity and Speed which based on Winford's model are "essentially Stative" in that they are incompatible with Imperfective aspect in JC. Items in these semantic classes seem for the most part to denote Stativity but as with the case of Physical Property items, there are some exceptions which suggest a need to look more closely at the categorisation presented by Winford. The examples below show lexical items from the categories Dimension, Colour, Age Human Propensity and Speed which display behaviour typical of these groups since, as indicated, these are expected not to be compatible with Non-stative meaning:

(22)   (Dimension) Jamaican Creole

    a. Di   riva **waid/lang/braad**.[11]
        ART river wide/long/broad
        'The river is wide/long/broad.'

    b. * Di   riva a   **waid/lang/braad**.
        ART river ASP wide/long/broad
        'The river is widening/lengthening/broadening.'

    c. * Dem a   **waid/lang/braad** di   riva.
        3PL ASP wide/long/broad ART river
        'They are widening/lengthening/broadening the river.'

---

[10] Non-stative expression for such items are available through the use of the semi-copula form *get* or by means of the morphological operation which adds the suffix *-op* thus creating a complex morphological verb (cf.: *di mango saaf-op/di mango get saaf* 'the mango got soft') however, these have no immediate relevance to this discussion.

[11] As will be discussed in Chapter 5, categorisation of these items may differ across speech communities; note for example that the similar form *bradi* in Sranan may appear in both Stative and Non-stative use. Also, there are indications of variability in its behaviour in JC as well.

3.4 Winford's semantic categorisation of CEC property items and an evaluation

    d. *Di uman a **fat**.
       ART woman ASP fat
       'The woman is getting fat.'

(23) (Colour) Jamaican Creole

    a. Di graas **griin**.
       ART grass green
       'The grass is green.'

    b. *Di graas a **griin**.
       ART grass ASP green
       'The grass is getting green.'

    c. *Mi faada **griin** di graas.
       1SG POSS father greean ART grass
       'My father made the grass green.'

(24) (Value) Jamaican Creole

    a. di plies **nais**.
       ART place nice
       'The place is nice.'

    b. *Di plies a **nais**.
       ART place ASP nice
       'The place is becoming nice.'

    c. *Dem **nais** di plies.
       3PL nice ART place
       'They made the place (look) nice.'

(25) (Age) Jamaican Creole

    a. Mi kluoz dem **uol**.
       1SG clothes PL old
       'My clothes are old.'

    b. *Mi kluoz dem a **uol**.
       1SG clothes PL ASP old
       'My clothes are getting old.'

    c. *Mi sista **uol** mi kluoz.
       1SG sister old 1SG clothes
       'My sister made my clothes old.'

3 The problem of dual aspectual forms

(26) (Human Propensity) Jamaican Creole

    a.   Da man de **chupid**.
        that man LOC stupid
        'That man is stupid.'

    b. * Da man de a **chupid**.
        that man LOC ASP stupid
        'That man is getting/behaving stupid.'

    c. * Di uman **chupid** di man.
        the woman stupid ART man
        'The woman made the man stupid.'

(27) (Speed) Jamaican Creole

    a.   Di kontri bos dem **sluo**.
        the country bus PL slow
        'The buses from the rural areas are slow.'

    b. * Di kontri bos dem a **sluo**.
        the country bus PL ASP slow
        'The buses from the rural areas are getting slow.'

    c. * Di bad ruod dem **sluo** di kontri bos dem.
        the bad road PL slow the country bus PL
        'The bad roads make the buses from the rural areas slow.'

The examples (22–27) above show JC items *waid/lang/braad* 'wide/long/broad', *griin* 'green', *uol* 'old', *nais* 'nice', *chupid* 'stupid' and *sluo* 'slow' which fall into the categories Dimension, Colour, Age, Value, Human propensity and Speed respectively in Stative use. As shown as well, these items are defiant to Non-stative expression as shown in the (b) and (c) examples where attempts at Imperfective aspect and transitive variation are made. Although they may express this by means of the semi-copula form *get* or by means of the morphological operation which adds the suffix *-op* or *dung* (up/down) thus creating a complex morphological verb, this is not immediately relevant to the present discussion and will not be addressed. Essentially, what these examples indicate is that such items at least in JC are not conceived as inherently involving a Change of state.

Based on Winford's classification, the behaviour of items from these categories is not particularly noteworthy as this is consistent with his expectations. However, as in the case of items falling into the category expressing Physical Property,

3.4 Winford's semantic categorisation of CEC property items and an evaluation

there are some notable exceptions that question the observational adequacy of Winford's model. Items of interest in this regard include *blak* 'black', *red* 'red' from the group expressing Colour, *bad/ruud* 'bad/rude' from the category expressing Value/Human Propensity, and *jelas* 'jealous', and *mad* 'mad', from the group expressing Human Propensity. As shown below, these items allow for Non-stative interpretations to varying degrees in contrast to what may be said to be the typical behaviour of items in their semantic group. Compare:

(28) Jamaican Creole (Colour)

    a.   di   skert **red/blak**.
           ART skirt red/black
           'The skirt is red/black.'

    b. ?? di   skert a   **red/blak**.
           ART skirt ASP red/black
           'The skirt is getting red/black.'

    c. ?? dem **red/blak** di   skert.
           3PL red/black ART skirt
           'They made the skirt red/black.'
           also 'They reddened/blackened the skirt.'

As indicated here, items such as *red* 'red', and *blak* 'black' from the category expressing Colour may be marginally acceptable in Non-stative use in JC. However, there are particular instances where these items are clearly acceptable in Non-stative use. Compare (29) which was heard uttered in a context where the sun was attributed with the change in colour seen in a mango on a tree as opposed to a natural state of ripeness:

(29) Di   son **red** di   mango.
     ART sun red ART mango
     'The sun reddened the mango/made the mango red.'

In Non-stative use, the interpretation of items such as 'red' and 'black' is that of a Change from one State to another. I will discuss the semantic implications of this in Chapter 5. It will become apparent that the Non-stative meaning indicated by these items is distinct from that which is expressed through items of the type *ded* 'dead', suggesting that there is a need to pay closer attention to the semantic interpretation that arises as opposed to simply the fact that an item appears in Non-stative use.

3 The problem of dual aspectual forms

The examples in (30) show another instance where Non-stative interpretation is allowed (unexpectedly based on Winford's model), and where the interpretation is distinct from that of a Change of state, which represents Winford's Non-stativity:

(30) (Value/Human Propensity) Jamaican Creole

    a. Da pikni de **bad/ruud**.
       that child DEM bad/rude
       'That child is (a) bad/rude (child).'

    b. Dat pikni de a **bad/ruud** (lang taim).
       that child DEM ASP bad/rude long time
       'That child has been misbehaving for a long time.'

Here we see items such as *bad* 'bad' and *ruud* 'rude' appearing with Non-stative interpretations but not expressing a Change from one State to another. In fact, what may be said to be expressed in the Non-stative use of these items is Process which does not result in a Change of state (i.e.: action associated with being bad or rude). This is similar to the meaning expressed by *jelas* 'jealous' in (31):

3.4 Winford's semantic categorisation of CEC property items and an evaluation

(31) Jamaican Creole

    a. Dem jealous.
       3PL   jealous
       'They are jealous.'

    b. Dem a   **jelas**   mi fi di kyar we mi jraiv.
       3PL ASP jealous 1SG for ART car that 1SG drive
       'They are (being) jealous/envious of me because of the car that I drive.'

In the example in (b) the lexical item *jelas* 'jealous' appears in Non-stative use to signal a meaning which points to actions associated with a particular state (jealousy/envy). Such usage is not accounted for in Winford's categorisation of property items which distinguishes Change of state verbs and Stative verbs.

The case of *mad* 'mad' which also falls into the category of Human Propensity, is similarly able to appear in Non-stative use:

(32) (Human Propensity) Jamaican Creole

    a. Im **mad**.
       3SG mad
       'He is crazy.'

    b. im a   **mad**.
       3SG ASP mad
       'He is going crazy.'

    c. A uman   **mad** im.
       is woman mad 3SG
       '(It's) A woman (that) drove him crazy.'

As shown in (32), *mad* 'mad' appears in the full range of Non-stative uses; allowing for both Imperfective aspect and transitive use. This, again, is a-typical of items in this semantic category, which based on Winford's model, are expected to be Stative and "behave like stative verbs" (p. 188). What the examples in (30–32) point to is a level of variation in the expression of Stativity among property items that is not just across semantic categories but even within these.

The aspectual behaviour evident in this group of items, based on this brief examination of JC data, indicates that there is more variation among property items than Winford noted. The extent of this variation does not allow for a treatment of particular items as exceptions to the rule but rather points to the need for a different model. In particular, it may not be possible to generalise over the behaviour

3 The problem of dual aspectual forms

of lexical items in these groups – at least not based on their membership in semantic classes Winford distinguishes. I propose to observe specific behaviours and focus on accounting for these from an Event Structure perspective.

3.5 Summary of observations

The problem presented by property items and dual aspectual forms in particular may be summed up as follows: the diversity of this group of items. This is apparent in both the discussion of the aspectual and categorial status of these items. As it relates to categorial status, items appear in both verbal and adjectival uses leading authors to seek an account that selects one category while explaining away the other (cf. Sebba 1986; Seuren 1986). Others may, as Kouwenberg (1996) does, posit a status for this group of items that includes both verbs and adjectives.

The former approaches have the immediate drawback of analysing this group of items as monolithic (verbs or adjectives), thereby not recognising the diversity that is apparent in their behaviour. From this perspective, these may be judged to be more subjective in their analyses where Kouwenberg (1996) may be seen as more objective in her treatment since she recognises this diversity and attempts to account for it. Nevertheless, none of these approaches achieve an understanding of what it is that accounts for the variation in behaviour that we see within this group of items.

In terms of the aspectual status of these items, it is apparent first of all that within the context of the Stative/Non-stative distinction, there is a large number of items which appear in Non-stative use along with their Stative uses. While Winford (1993) claims a split in the aspectual status of these items based on semantic groups (i.e., items expressing Physical Property as Non-stative as opposed to all others as Stative), observation of JC data shows that items which appear in Non-stative use are not restricted to the semantic group of Physical Property as indicated by Winford. Rather, items displaying this flexibility in usage range across his semantic categories and display different subtypes of Non-stative meaning, including Change of state (e.g., *ded* 'dead', colour items), and Process (e.g., *ruud* 'rude', *bad* 'bad', *jelas* 'jealous').

The different aspectual interpretations associated with property items in Non-stative use indicate that we are dealing with different types of items. Based on the preliminary evaluation above, it seems that there are at least three different classes of items in this group: First, items of the type *ded* 'dead' and also those expressing Colour like *red* 'red' and *blak* 'black' which appear in Stative and Non-stative use and which, in the latter use, indicate a Change of state. Secondly those of the type *chupid* 'stupid', *saaf* 'soft', *haad* 'hard', *swiit* 'sweet' etc., which do not appear in Non-stative use. And thirdly those of the type *jelas* 'jealous' and *bad* 'bad' which, like the first group of items, appear in both Stative and Non-stative use, but do not indicate a Change from one state to another but rather an ongoing Process. Chapter 4 will set the background for the classification of these items based on an Event Structure that I will elaborate in subsequent chapters.

In the treatment that I espouse the question of the categorial status is addressed as secondary in relation to aspectual status. However, as we will see in Chapters 5 and 6 in particular, there is a logical relation between the two issues, such that an understanding of aspectual behaviour provides insights into categorial status. In the chapters which follow, I will seek to account for the diversity that is expressed in the behaviour of property items. First by exploring what is indicated by the Stative/Non-stative distinction and what would account for a single item which is able to express both these meanings. It will become apparent that one may not be able to generalise over the behaviour of specific property items across Creoles. Nevertheless, there is a level at which the categorisation of an item and its actual behaviour can be understood in an appropriate model based on event types. From such a perspective it may be possible to offer an account of CEC property items from a more universal perspective while allowing for a language-specific categorisation of these items.

4 The Stative/Non-stative distinction and change as a lexico-semantic concept

4.1 Introduction

In this chapter I will discuss Change as the abstract semantic concept associated with the notions of Stativity [−Change] and Non-stativity [+Change]. Even though this concept of Change is not generally formalised in the literature on Aspect, discussions more often than not are pervaded by this concept as a way to distinguish between two main classes of verbs – Stative/Non-stative. Verkuyl (1996; 1999), may be accredited with positing [+/−Change] as a feature distinguishing verbs based on the Stative/Non-stative opposition. However, many authors including Vendler (1967); Comrie (1976); Mourelatos (1981); Jackendoff (1996) and Krifka (1998) have made reference to this notion of Change as a basic concept associated with situations. In general, the discussion has not surrounded whether or not there are verbs that express Change and those which do not but rather the complexity of Change, especially in the context of the compositionality of Aspect. Thus, for example authors such as Verkuyl (1996; 1999); Tenny (1994); Jackendoff (1996) and Krifka (1998; 2001) while not principally focused on the verb itself, are concerned with how Change in the verb interacts with other elements to impact Telicity.

In my opinion, the case of dual aspectual items in CECs and the discussion of them that has developed places focus on the verb itself and the applicability of what may be seen as a distinction that captures a basic intuition – the Stative/Non-stative distinction. Here, I will attempt to address the question of the unique aspectual contribution of verbs[1] to Aspect despite items which appear to express dual aspects. As indicated (Chapter 1), the idea of an aspectual value associated with verbs must be taken within the context of the compositionality of Aspect,

---

[1] The items under discussion function dually as adjectives and verbs, thus using the label verbs here is not intended to imply a different categorisation.

4 The Stative/Non-stative distinction and change as a lexico-semantic concept

and in the approach that I take both concepts are seen as compatible. Essentially, if the verb is accepted as a part of this composition, it seems reasonable to assume that there is a basic value associated with this element even if it may be impacted and modified through interaction with other elements in composition.

In the approach that I take here, the notion of inherent aspect is reduced to the concept of Change, with its origin in the lexico-semantic representation of verbs. Despite what seems to be a simplification of Vendler's (1967) four classes of verbs (i.e., Activity, Accomplishment, Achievement and State), the concept of Change itself is shown below to be quite complex. Change is taken to be composed of different (combinations of) primitives consistent with the contrasts observed in the behaviour of different verbs in transitivity alternations as highlighted in the work of Levin (1993). In the exploration of the semantic concept of Change that I undertake here, I identify primitives such as CAUSE and DO, and also BECOME (see McCawley 1968; Carter 1988; Dowty 1979) as those relevant in the discussion of dual aspectual forms in CECs.

As I will outline in my analysis of dual aspectual forms in Chapter 5, the presence of a primitive such as CAUSE (in conjunction with BECOME) is responsible for the presence of a Cause as seen in the transitive (Non-stative) expression of JC items such as *raip* 'make ripe', *sik* 'make sick', *redi* 'make ready', etc. I argue, however, that it is the introduction of either CAUSE + BECOME or BECOME in the Event Structure of items such as *blak* 'black' that accounts for the transitive and inchoative realisation of such items. In a similar way, DO accounts for the introduction of Agency in the Non-stative use of items such as *jelas* 'act jealously' or *bad* 'misbehave'. Seminal works concerned with verb meanings and primitive structures will be a point of focus in the discussion that ensues. Thus, while I assume, like contemporary authors such as Verkuyl (1999); Tenny (1994); Tenny & Pustejovsky (2000); Rothstein (2004); MacDonald (2008) etc., that Aspect is compositional (see Chapter 1 for discussion), the earlier works of McCawley (1968); Carter (1988); Dowty (1979); Pustejovsky (1988; 1991) and Grimshaw (1990) will be the ones surveyed here.

Significantly, these earlier works focused on the nature of verb meaning, whereas the more contemporary authors assumed a basic contribution of the verb in the composition of Aspect without focusing on the nature of this element per se. A bias towards these earlier works is in line with my focus on the verb and interest in accounting for the different uses in which property items appear. The more contemporary among these earlier works (Pustejovsky 1988; 1991 and Grimshaw 1990) will provide a model of Event Structure that accounts for the ability of (inherently) dual aspectual forms to appear in the uses that they do and with their associated meanings. The earlier decompositions of McCawley (1968); Carter (1988) and Dowty (1979) elucidate the significance of primitives and thus supply a background for the identification of the specific type of primitive meanings that are applicable in the Non-stative contrasts among property items. This is particularly relevant in accounting for the semantic difference between inherent (Non-stative) dual aspectual items and those whose dual aspectual behaviour results from morphological derivation.

The chapter is organised as follows: In §4.2 I will outline the basic notion of an inherent aspectual contribution of the verb to Aspect in the form of Comrie's State/Non-state distinction. In §4.3, I will explore lexico-semantic structures representing Change and the significance of this notion by looking at the different types and structures associated with events (§4.3.1), the primary primitives of Change (§4.3.2) and transitivity alternations (§4.3.3). The discussion coming out of this chapter will form the basis for the analysis of dual aspectual forms in CECs in Chapter 5.

4.2 The stative/non-stative distinction and the notion of Change

Comrie (1976) in his discussion of Aspect, contrasts the verb *know* with *run* to highlight the Static/Dynamic (also State/Non-state) distinction. He points to a verb such as *know* as not involving Change, in contrast to *run* which involves "necessary Change" (p. 49). Regarding the State/Non-state distinction, Comrie comments that it is:

> one that seems reasonably clear intuitively, and in practice one finds a large measure of agreement between individuals who are asked to classify situations as static or dynamic. (p. 48)

A key term in his description of this opposition is the term "phase" which allows one to look into the situation as it relates to the notion of Change. Essentially, in the case of a verb such as *know* (State), he points out that

> all phases of the situation *John knows where I live* are identical; whichever point of time we choose to cut in on the situation of John's knowledge, we shall find exactly the same situation. (p. 49)

In the case of the verb *run* (dynamic) however, he points out that this is not so: if we say *John is running,* then different phases of the situation will be very different: at one moment John will have one foot on the ground, at another moment neither foot will be on the ground and so on. Thus *know* on the one hand involves no Change whereas *run* involves necessarily Change. (p. 49)

While there are situations captured in this opposition that may not be so straightforward, the key element here is the notion of "necessary Change." As Comrie points out, while there may be Stative situations that *may* involve Change, dynamic situations involve "necessary Change" (p. 49). I take this to refer to the inherent meaning components of the verb. It is along these lines that I now explore the notion of Change as an abstract semantic concept in these sections.

The intuition regarding the State/Non-state opposition as viewed by Comrie is that this distinction captures the inherent meaning of the verb rather than that of the VP (the verb and internal argument). Also, differences in the semantic content of the internal argument (see discussion in Chapter 1) will not/cannot trigger a change in the nature of the verb itself from indicating Change to not doing so. I provide the examples below showing the verbs *know* and *run* as consistently expressing [−Change] and [+Change][2] respectively (by default), in spite of the influence of an internal argument:

(1) (personal examples)[3]

    a. John **knows** (Stative)

    b. John **knows** the answer. (Stative)

    c. John **knew** the answer. (Stative)

(2)   a. John **runs** (Non-stative)

    b. John **runs** a mile. (Non-stative)

    c. John **ran** a mile. (Non-stative)

---

[2] This feature [+/−Change] is also used by Verkuyl (1999) to capture the contribution of the verb to Aspect in his compositional model. This is noteworthy given the fact that Verkuyl argues against a lexical division of verbs. What this shows is that the idea of a unique aspectual contribution of the verb to Aspect is not opposed to Aspect as compositional; it is however a matter of identifying the unique contribution of each element and of identifying how the different elements interact.

[3] What I posit here are default interpretations. I am fully aware of the effect that factors such as context and adverbials may have on such default interpretations especially in the case of the verb *know* (cf.: *John knew immediately!*). Since my intention is to capture as far as possible a default (inherent) meaning associated with the verb, the possible influence of other factors in these examples is not considered.

4.2 The stative/non-stative distinction and the notion of Change

The examples in (1) show the verb *know* appearing in the Present Tense without an internal argument (1a), with a specified internal argument (1b) and in Past Tense with a specified internal argument. In all these cases, the default interpretation of the verb *know* may be said to not indicate any kind of Change. In contrast, in the case of *run* in (2), the default interpretation associated with this verb is one that includes Change specifically in terms of motion.

One difference that we may note among the Non-statives here is that while (2a) may be used to refer to a situation with no specified end time (Habitual or Generic in this case Atelic), both (2b) and (2c) refer to situations having a fixed end point and as such are both Telic. In this sense, using Vendler's (1967) terminology widely adopted in the literature, (2a) may be called an Activity while (2b) and (2c) are Accomplishments. In the usage that I employ here the notions of Activity and Accomplishment refer to the aspect established at VP rather than the denotation of the verb itself. In this way, the basic contribution of the verb as indicating Change or not is separated from any additional influence brought about by the internal argument, grammatical aspect or other elements.

The notion of Change applied in the sense above may be seen as an abstract semantic concept in that, while it may not be either morphologically or syntactically expressed, it has semantic force. Thus for example, in (3) below as opposed to (4) some (physical) Change in terms of the situation conveyed by the verb must be conceived:

(3) (personal examples)

    a. John **runs** that race every year.

    b. John **eats** mom's dinner every evening.

    c. John **blinks** his left eye every ten minutes .

(4) a. John **knows** everyone at school.

    b. John **has** a better mentor.

Consistent with Comrie's association of "necessary change" in the conceptualisation of Non-stative as opposed to Stative verbs, we note here that the meanings associated with the examples in (3) involve "necessary change" as opposed to those in (4) where no "necessary change" is expressed.

In order for (3a) to be true, movement/motion must be accepted to take place upon each occurrence of the event of *running*. In this case, John is both the Agent and the entity that is affected (Agent and Theme as Pustejovsky (1988: 28) notes). Through Change instantiated by motion, John is translated from one point to the next. The race is simply the domain in which the event takes place and it provides a measure for the event. In the case of (3b), there is a Change that affects the internal argument (in this case *mom's dinner*) whereby it is changed from its original complete state by being consumed. In (3c) the action of *blinking* indicates that there is a (momentary) Change of state and a return to the original State. Thus each situation expressed in (3) involves Change. In the case of (4) however, there is no "necessary change" for these to be true. One may be able to imagine a time before when the statement *John knows everyone at school* or *John has a better mentor* was not true but the verbs in question *know* and *have* do not capture a Change from a previous state to the one in question; only the state of affairs as it exists for the period in question.

So far in this discussion, I have presented the notion of Change as an abstract semantic notion. In the section below I will look at the primitives that are associated with the expression of Change.

4.3 Event structures and primitives of change

The difference between Stative and Non-stative predicates has been captured in models of lexico-semantic representations through the use of primitives (Mc-Cawley 1968; Carter 1988; Dowty 1979; Jackendoff 1996; etc.) and Event Structure representations (Pustejovsky 1988; 1991; Grimshaw 1990). With regard to the latter, Pustejovsky (1988; 1991) and Grimshaw (1990) identify three event types and a separation between State on one hand and Non-state-Transition and Process on the other.

Overall, States are characterized by the absence of primitives associated with Change while Non-states are defined by different (combinations of) primitives associated with Change. The primary primitives associated with Change are BE-COME and CAUSE which signal inchoative Change and Change through an external Cause respectively. Other primitives such as DO (see Dowty 1979) and GO (Jackendoff 1996) have been discussed in reference to verbs of Agency and motion (both Process verbs). The discussion of transitivity alternations (Levin (1993) also highlights primitives such as MOTION, CONTACT, and CHANGE OF STATE as relevant in accounting for the behaviour of different types of verbs.

In the sections which follow, I will look at three main areas as it relates to the discussion of Change as a semantic concept: In §4.3.1, I will look at the three types of structures that characterise events. In §4.3.2, I will look at the primary primitives associated with Change and taken to be relevant in the case of dual aspectual forms in CECs. These, are primarily CAUSE, BECOME and DO. I use these

4.3 Event structures and primitives of change

concepts in Chapter 5 to account in particular for the derived Non-stative use of items such as JC *blak* 'black' and *red* 'red' in inchoative and transitive use. Specifically the introduction of a primitive such as BECOME accounts for the inchoative use of these item while BECOME + CAUSE account for their transitive use. DO is the primitive that is relevant in the case of the Processual expression of *jelas* 'jealous' and *bad* 'bad', I summarise this discussion of Change as a semantic concept by looking at the relevance of Change as indicated by transitivity alternations in §4.3.3.

4.3.1 Event types and structures

Event Structures capture the differences between predicates expressing Change and those which do not. Representations such as those of Pustejovsky (1988; 1991) and Grimshaw (1990) show a difference between States and Non-states in the structure of sub-events (e_1 and e_2). Non-states are identified as associated with a first sub-event associated with Causation and Change while pure States are captured in representation not associated with Change. Based on the representations of these authors, there are three types of Event Structures: State on one hand and Process/Activity and Transition on the other. According to Pustejovsky (1988),

> the grammar specifies three primitive event-types: *state, process, transition*. A verb is identified as having one of these event-types associated with it lexically. Furthermore, all eventuality-denoting sentences in the language must conform to one of these templates. (p. 22)

Seen from this perspective, not only is the notion of event type associated with verbs but also with sentences. In this regard, Pustejovsky (1991) notes "[b]ecause an event structure is recursively defined in the syntax, "event-type" is also a property of phrases and sentences." (p. 55). This essentially means that Event Structure is redefined within the context of the interaction of other aspectual elements within the syntactic domain. In this way, it takes into consideration the lexical contribution of the verb as well as the compositionality of Aspect. Below I will look at the different event types in turn; these will later be applied to an analysis of CEC dual aspectual forms in Chapter 5.

4.3.2 State

A State according to Pustejovsky (1991) is a "single event which is evaluated relative to no other event" (p. 56). This is shown in Figure 4.1.

4 The Stative/Non-stative distinction and change as a lexico-semantic concept

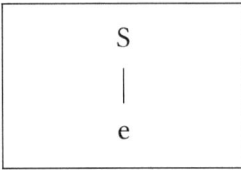

Figure 4.1: State: A single event evaluated relative to no other event (Pustejovsky 1991: 56)

The Event Structure in Figure 4.1 is associated with lexical items such as *be sick, love, know* etc. based on Pustejovsky (1991).[4] As the representation shows, a State (S) is an event (e) that exists as inherently unrelated to any other event. This representation in Figure 4.1 may be compared with Jackendoff (1996) which presents a State as a situation which "just sits there with no dependence on time – only a location in time" (p. 327). Jackendoff's representation of a canonical State is thus of a situation in time that is not spatially bound to time on an axis. What this means essentially is that there is no dependence between the time constituent and the structure of the situation. His representation is shown in Figure 4.2.

$$[_{Sit} F(X,Y); [_{Time} T]]$$
(where 'Sit' = Situation)

Figure 4.2: Canonical State (Jackendoff 1996: 327)

Using the conceptual idea of a rotating axis, Jackendoff presents the movement of a situation in time as related to the Changes in the situation for Non-stative situation (Events). This representation shows that the continuation of this situation (State) in time is not affected by time as there is no axis binding the two.

Although the representations in Figures 4.1 and 4.2 are schematically different, they capture the basic intuition that I apply in relation to CEC property items and dual aspectual forms, which is that a State is not associated with Change. In the analysis of CEC dual aspectual items the concept of State will be important in accounting for items that do not allow for Non-stative use. It also extends items which do appear in Non-stative use but do so, as I will argue, through the introduction of primitives associated with Change rather than due to their inherent lexical composition.

---

[4] I do not necessarily assume the same categorisation for similar lexical items in CECs. For example as will be seen in §5.3 the categorisation of an item such as *sik* 'sick/become sick/sicken' based on its behaviour is that of a Transition rather than a State.

4.3 Event structures and primitives of change

4.3.3 Transition

A Transition is one of the two event types which are characterised by Change. The Event Structure representing it shows an event that is evaluated relative to another event, entailing a State and a Process (Change of state). This is shown in Figure 4.3.

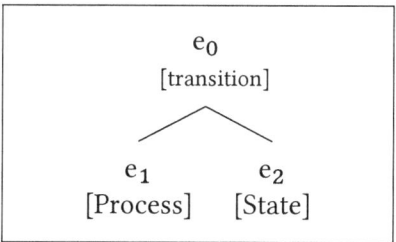

Figure 4.3: Event Structure of Transition

A Transition as shown here is an event (e_0) constituting two events (e_1, e_2) which are evaluated relative to each other. The first event (e_1) represents a Change of state (Process) and the second event (e_2) represents the result of this Change of state (State). A lexical item associated with this Event Structure based on Pustejovsky (1991) is *close*.

The difference between the State that forms a part of a Transition Event Structure and the pure State shown in Figure 4.2 is that the former is linked to a Process as shown in Figure 4.3, whilst a pure State does not encode such a relation. It is important to note as well that the Process involved in a Transition Event Structure is distinct from that of a pure Process in that it has a logical opposition with which it is inherently linked. According to Pustejovsky (1991), a Transition is "an event identifying a semantic expression, which is evaluated relative to its opposition" (p. 56). The concept of a Transition Event Structure will be used to account for CEC property items which appear in Non-stative use expressing an opposition between contrarieties. This notion of opposition will be crucial in differentiating between derived and inherent Transitions. I elaborate this in §5.3.

4.3.4 Process

The Event Structure of Process represents what may be seen as an ongoing event characterised by Change. Unlike a Transition, however, it is not evaluated relative to another event (i.e., a logical result). According to Pustejovsky (1991) it is identified as "a sequence of events identifying the same semantic expression" (p. 56). The structure representing this is shown in Figure 4.4:

4 The Stative/Non-stative distinction and change as a lexico-semantic concept

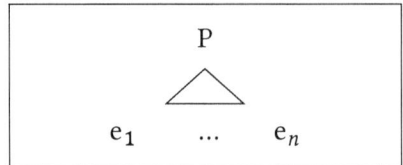

Figure 4.4: Process Event Structure (Pustejovsky 1991: 56)

Some verbs that are noted as associated with this Event Structure are *run, push, drag*, etc. (Pustejovsky 1991: 56). Such verbs bear out what Tenny (1994) refers to as the Measuring Out Constraint (MOC) on direct internal arguments. The MOC is a constraint that addresses the interaction between the "direct internal argument" and a "simple verb". Within this interaction, according to Tenny (1994),

> [t]he direct internal argument [...] is constrained so that it undergoes no necessary internal motion or change, unless it is motion or change which 'measures out the event' over time. (p. 11)

Necessary motion or change as indicated by Tenny (1994) means that this is "required by the verb's meaning" (ibid). Thus she points out for the sentence *John ate the apple up* that it

> describes an event in which the apple is necessarily changed by being consumed. John might also be changed by becoming full, but that is not required in an interpretation of the sentence. John may or may not become full, but the apple must be consumed. (p. 11–12)

This constraint which may be associated with a Process distinguishes this Event Structure from that of a Transition in that the structure shows a continuous event but no logical result except that associated with the progression of the event itself. Thus, it may be said that in the process of eating, something is necessarily consumed as the event progresses but this event is not inherently associated with a (resultant) State outside of this context. The event type of Process will be useful in accounting for the derived (Non-stative) use of items such as *jelas, bad* and *ruud* as I discuss in §5.3.3.

Jackendoff (1996) criticises Tenny (1994) and Pustejovsky (1991) among others for the "snapshot" conceptualisation indicated by the Event Structure representation in Figure 4.4 and the explanations associated with the notion of Process. He observes that these authors present a Process and in particular an event of motion as "a series of snapshots, each which depicts the object of motion in a

4.3 Event structures and primitives of change

different location" (p. 315–316). He rejects this view, primarily on the grounds that it "misrepresents the essential continuity of events of motion" (p. 316). In his approach, he presents a conceptualisation where "instead of treating motion as a finite sequence of states" it is presented as "continuous change over time" (p. 317). Based on this, he represents a Process event as projected onto axes where

> there are three axes to consider at once: the point situation is projected onto a durative event [...] the point in space is projected onto a path; and the point in time is projected onto a time interval (p. 321)

His representation is shown in Figure 4.5.

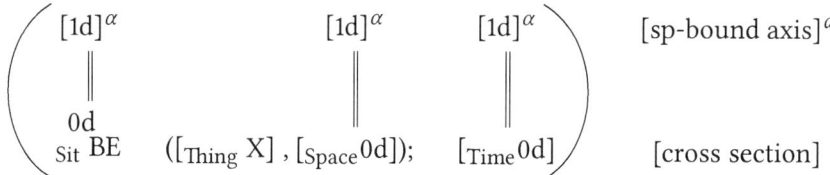

Figure 4.5: Jackendoff's (1996: 322) Process

---

[a]Refers to the structure-preserving (sp-)binding relationship between Situation, Path and Time axes (Jackendoff 1996: 322)

As shown here, a Process is presented as three axes (the Situation, represented by BE, Space, and Time) which are joined to each other in such a way that any progression associated with one, effects progression in the others. In such a representation, Jackendoff points out that "measuring out is a consequence of the sp-binding of the path event and time axes" (p. 323).

Jackendoff's representation serves to capture the intuitions of authors such as Pustejovsky (1991); Krifka (1998), Tenny (1994); Verkuyl (1996) etc., especially as it relates to Telicity effects. Nevertheless, in my discussion of CEC property items in Chapter 5, I will make use of the basic Event Structure representing a Process employed by Pustejovsky (1991) to account for CEC property items which express Non-stativity consistent with the meaning "behave in accordance with X quality". As I argue in §5.3.2, such items are inherently associated with a State Event Structure, however, they are derived to express a Process. In this manner, they are distinct from items inherently associated with the Event Structure of Process, which do not also appear in Stative use.

In the sections below, I will look at the different primitives of Change that may be said to be active in and relevant to the Event Structures of Transition

4 The Stative/Non-stative distinction and change as a lexico-semantic concept

and Process. Note that States are distinguished by the absence of any primitive associated with Change.

4.4 Primitives of Change

The discussion in this section will indicate that the systematic difference in aspectual meaning between the Stative and Non-stative use of dual aspectual forms may be linked to the presence or introduction of particular semantic primitives associated with the aspectual feature, Change. This analysis is consistent with the view that "words are not unanalyzed atoms but can be decomposed into a set of recurrent conceptual features or traits" (Chierchia & McConnell-Ginet 1992: 350). This view provides an understanding of the uses of JC *raip*. For example, although there is no overt morphological difference between *raip* 'ripe' that expresses a State and *raip* 'ripe' that denotes a Process, in terms of aspect they denote [–Change] in one instance and [+Change] in another. Thus, in the case of (5a), there is only an indication of the State of ripeness consistent with the expression of the feature [–Change]. However, in (5b), there is an indication of this State coming about [+Change]. This is made explicit through the presence of the Progressive aspect marker. Note also that (5c) shows the presence of a Cause or Agent:

(5) a. di planten **raip**.
ART plantain ripe
'The plantain is ripe.'

b. di planten a **raip**.
ART plantain ASP ripe
'The plantain is getting ripe.'

c. dem **raip** di planten.
3PL ripe ART plantain
'They ripen the plantain.'

What I identify in these instances are different realizations of the same lexical item based on the elements of meanings that are present as a part of its conceptual structure at the lexico-semantic level.

Hence, an analysis of an item such as *raip* 'ripe' is expected to reveal elements of meaning consistent with the different interpretations of this item at the surface level. A composite of semantic primitives associated with a particular item provides a basis for its different expressions. This, in essence, is consistent with

4.4 Primitives of Change

the view that the behaviour of an item is determined by its meaning (Levin 1993: 1). In the sections below, I will look specifically at the primitives BECOME, CAUSE and DO. These are the primitives which I use to account for the expression of Non-stativity among property items in Chapter 5.

4.4.1 BECOME and CAUSE

The primitives BECOME and CAUSE have been used in the literature to capture an internal Change of state (BECOME) or a Change of state brought about by a Cause (CAUSE + BECOME). Both primitives appear in McCawley's (1968) decomposed representation of the lexical item *kill*. BECOME is used to show the relation between the opposition ALIVE and DEAD and the Transition between these results in the meaning associated with the English lexical item *to die*. The introduction of the primitive CAUSE in the same configuration accounts for the difference in meaning between 'die' and 'kill' which is one of Causation. This is shown below:

(6) 'Kill' (adapted from McCawley 1968: 73)

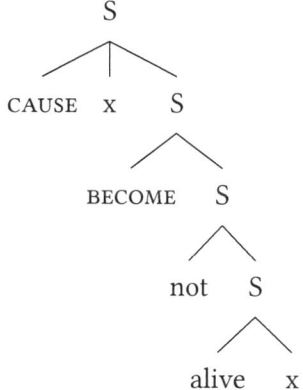

Based on this representation, the meaning of the verb *kill* is made to contain the Stative meanings 'alive' and 'dead/not alive' as well as the Non-stative meanings 'die', 'kill' or 'CAUSE to BECOME not alive', McCawley's approach to decomposition is rooted in the syntax-semantics interface where it is believed that semantic regularities whether or not they coincide with actual words in the lexicon may be encoded in the syntax in terms of grammatical relations in the expression of certain meanings. According to McCawley (1973), the primitives in his representation are not features of the sentence but are "relations between items of content that figure in the sentence" (p. 344). In other words, while the primitives themselves will not appear in the sentence, they are related to the appearance of items that appear in the sentence.

For example, although *kill* itself would appear as a single word in a sentence, its decompositional content shows a relationship with its argument structure and accounts for the fact that this item appears in a transitive structure including a Patient as internal argument and a Cause/Agent in the external argument position. The appearance of this Cause/Agent is licensed by the CAUSE primitive in the conceptual structure of the lexical item. This primitive distinguishes the transitive and Non-stative verb *kill* from words with otherwise similar meanings associated with 'dead' (i.e., not ALIVE), and the inchoative 'die' (i.e., BECOME not ALIVE) which McCawley took to be part of the composite of the verb *kill*. Unlike *kill* which has a Causative element of meaning, their lexico-semantic structures are presented as licensing only a patient argument and this is what we see reflected in the syntactic domain.

The logical relation between the lexical items corresponding to the meanings 'CAUSE to BECOME not ALIVE' (i.e.: kill), 'BECOME not ALIVE' (i.e.: die) and 'not ALIVE' (i.e.: dead) where *kill* logically entails both the meanings of 'die' and 'dead', may be shown through examples such as (7):

(7) (personal examples)

    a. Mary killed the plants.

    b. The plants are dead [not ALIVE] (because Mary killed them).

    c. The plants died [BECOME not ALIVE] (because of Mary)

In (7), the example in (7a) entails both the meanings of (7b) and (7c). Essentially, if (7a) holds true then (7b) and (7c) are also true. The configuration in (6) captures this intuition and in this way may be said to appeal to a sense of semantic logic.

McCawley has, however, been criticised for this kind of decomposition as later authors point out that the representation in (6) does not coincide with the treatment of 'kill' in any of the world's languages. In this regard, Travis (2000) for example, who accepts the presence of a syntactic head where there is evidence for this in only one language, points out regarding *kill* that:

> Since no language [...] encodes *kill* with morphological bits meaning CAUSE BECOME NOT ALIVE, I believe that syntax has no right encoding all of these concepts (p. 182)

From this perspective, McCawley's representation may be analysed as misguided. However, what we can abstract from McCawley is the basic idea that word meaning may be broken down to reflect generalities and a connection between forms that are semantically related. Note also that current (Minimalist) Syntactic Theory assumes the presence of a "light verb" equivalent to CAUSE which licenses the external argument for any verb which takes an Agent or Cause as external argument. From this perspective the basic intuition captured by McCawley may be said to be vindicated.

McCawley's use of the primitives BECOME and CAUSE to indicate a Change of state and Causation respectively is also reflected in the work of Dowty (1979) and Carter (1988). As shown below, Dowty (1979) presents *He sweeps the floor clean* as a logical relationship between two propositions; [*He sweeps the floor*] and [*the floor is clean*]. These are joined by the primitives CAUSE and BECOME:

(8) (Dowty 1979: 93)
He sweeps the floor clean.
[[He sweeps the floor] CAUSE [BECOME [*the floor is clean*]]]

Dowty (1979) is similar to McCawley (1968) in his employment of CAUSE and BECOME as primitive notions associated with Change. Note however a conceptual separation of Cause from Agency in this representation which separates the action (Activity) [He sweeps the floor] from both the CAUSE and the resulting Change of state [*the floor is clean*]. In §4.3.2 below, I will look at his DO primitive which overtly captures this separation between Cause and Agency.

Carter (1988) also employs CAUSE as a primitive in his representation of an item such as DARKEN. Although he does not overtly present BECOME in his representation, this may be said to be captured in his use of CHANGE as a primitive. As shown below, Carter (1988) presents items such as DARK and DARKEN as morphologically related through a Causative primitive. Based on his representation the English form *darken* is a relation between CAUSE and the state BE DARK where the interaction points to the initiation of a Change of state:

(9) Carter's (1988: 6) representation of DARKEN
DARKEN: X CAUSE ((Y BE DARK) CHANGE)

Note here that CHANGE may be interpreted as a way of capturing the meaning of BECOME as the bracketing suggests as well that CHANGE is introduced before CAUSE. Carter's representation, different from McCawley's, includes the use of BE as a primitive associated with a State which is embedded under the Non-stative meanings. Based on the apparent differences in these representations, it may be useful to note a separation of notions associated with Change where CAUSE and BECOME may be seen as subtypes of the articulation of Change.

4 The Stative/Non-stative distinction and change as a lexico-semantic concept

Note that dark > darken is a morphological operation which changes the Event Structure – something which will turn out to be relevant to the analysis of CEC dual aspectual forms in Chapter 5. I will posit there that CEC forms indicating Colour may be distinguished among property items by being open to a morphological process similar to the one which Carter captures here.

4.4.2 DO

DO appears in the literature as a primitive which denotes Agency. I discuss it here as a primitive relevant to the case of those property items which, in derived Non-stative use, express a simple Process or Activity, as will be discussed in §5.3. Dowty (1979) points to this primitive in his overall discussion to account for the notion of volition (Agency) that distinguishes "actives" such as *listen to* and *watch* from the cognitives *hear* and *see*. Regarding the meaning associated with DO he points out that "a semantic factor which DO contributes is roughly the notion of volition (and/or intention), contemporaneous with the act on the part of the subject"[5] (p. 114). This definition is important in my decision to associate this primitive with the meaning seen in derived Processes in CECs.

In positing DO, Dowty (1979) separates it from CAUSE and BECOME on the basis of the lexical productivity of the latter primitives. In this regard, he states that,

> the evidence for DO is less persuasive than that arguing for CAUSE and BECOME, and the role played by DO in the aspect calculus is less significant than that played by CAUSE and BECOME. There is no productive word formation process "adding" a DO to a verb in English (much less in other languages I know of) as there is the case of CAUSE and BECOME in a large number of languages. (p. 119)

However, the case of CECs dual aspectual forms may provide some evidence for DO as a primitive associated with a productive process in the lexicon. This is based on the behaviour of items such as JC *jelas* 'jealous' and *bad* 'bad' which in Non-stative use express a Process (Activity) not resulting in a Change of state as opposed to the causative or inchoative interpretations associated with the Non-stative interpretations of other items. In Chapter 5, I discuss these in Non-stative use as possibly indicative of the introduction of the element of meaning DO. This is elaborated in my analysis in §5.3.

---

[5] The idea associated with this notion of "act on the part of the subject" is what I believe sets this primitive apart from one such as GO (Jackendoff 1972; 1996) which also expresses Agency but also includes motion.

4.5 More on Change: Transitivity alternations

Transitivity alternations have been discussed in the literature in relation to the different behaviours displayed by groups of verbs. The work of Levin (1993) is perhaps the most extensive so far and it will serve as my point of reference in this section. My focus here will be on how the presence or absence of elements of meaning associated with Change affect whether or not a verb may participate in a particular alternation. This I believe provides some tangible evidence of the syntactic relevance of Change which I have discussed so far as a semantic concept. As we will see, transitivity alternations do not express the Stative/Non-stative distinction as these alternations pertain only to Non-stative verbs. However, they may be said to point to the syntactic relevance of Change and also to the complexity of this abstract semantic notion in the way that the presence of particular elements of meanings allows for the participation of some verbs as opposed to others in these alternations.

As I outline in this section, transitivity alternations are determined based on the composite of primitives that are associated with some verbs as opposed to others. This is in line with Levin's (1993) observation that

> the behaviour of a verb, particularly with respect to the expression and interpretation of its argument is to a large extent determined by its meaning. (p. 1)

Jackendoff's (1975) observation that the first level of adequacy in language description "consists in providing each lexical item with sufficient information to describe its behavior in the language" (p. 639, cf. Chomsky 1965) is pertinent in this regard.

As we will see below, in the discussion of transitivity alternations, there is a separation among verbs based on the type of Change that they express. In the case of the middle and causative/inchoative alternations, the relevant primitives determining the participation of a verb are BECOME (and CAUSE) (discussed in §4.4.1). The body-part possessor ascension alternation highlights the relevance of the notion of CONTACT, while it is the combined notions of MOTION and CONTACT that are pertinent in the conative alternation. I will discuss these alternations in turn.

4 The Stative/Non-stative distinction and change as a lexico-semantic concept

4.5.1 CAUSE and BECOME in the middle and causative/inchoative alternations

The middle alternation allows for a generalisation to be made over the behaviour of an internal argument without the inclusion of a Cause or Agent in the expression. As shown below in (10) the verbs *cut* and *break* are distinct from others such as *touch* and *hit* in their ability to appear in the middle alternation. Compare (10):

(10) Restrictions on the middle alternation (Levin 1993: 6, example 13)

    a.   The bread **cuts** easily.
    b.   Crystal vases **break** easily.
    c.   * Cats **touch** easily.
    d.   * Door frames **hit** easily.

As seen here, a verb such as *break* or *cut* may appear in the middle alternation where this is not possible for a verb such as *touch* or *hit*. This is due to the presence of the element of meaning BECOME which points to a Change of state in the internal argument for verbs such as *cut* and *break* but not *touch* and *hit*.

The causative/inchoative alternation, also highlights the syntactic relevance of CAUSE and BECOME as primitives associated with Change. In this alternation, there is a separation between verbs which denote a Change of state in an internal argument without any implication of an external Cause or Agent and all others. As Levin (1993) points out, this variation applies to

> a pure change of state verb [...] denoting an entity undergoing a change of state [...] the two argument form of the verb found in the causative variant is derived by the addition of a notion of a cause. (p. 9–10)

Thus for example, there is evidence of a separation between verbs such as *roll, close* and *break* as opposed to *cut* in English which does not permit this alternation. Compare (11):

(11) Restrictions on the causative/inchoative alternation (my examples)

    a.   * The cloth **cut**.[6]
    b.   Mark **cut** the cloth.

---

[6] Though this is not a possibility in English, similar structures are salient in varieties of CECs e.g.: JC *Di klaat kot*. 'The cloth is/has been cut'. What this suggests is a difference in the semantic conceptualisation of such a form in CECs as opposed to their English lexifier or simply the availability of an unmarked passive (subject to constraints which are, as yet, unclear; see Allsopp 1983).

c. The ball **rolled**.
d. The boy **rolled** the ball.
e. The door **closed**.
f. The boy/the wind **closed** the door.
g. The window **broke**.
h. The boy/the wind **broke** the window.

As noted here, items such as *roll*, *close*, and *break* allow for the causative/inchoative variation. These constitute the class of unaccusative verbs which may be used Non-statively with no implication of a Cause or Agent. The semantics of these verbs include the notion of BECOME (consistent with a Change of state) without the inherent involvement of a Cause or Agent. The introduction of a Cause or Agent accounts for the causative variations of these verbs. The causative/inchoative variation is thus restricted to verbs which allow for a separation between a Cause and a Change of state. This is not the case for a verb like *cut* in English, as a Change of state in the internal argument seems to be linked inherently to the action of a Cause or Agent.

4.5.2 CONTACT in the body-part possessor ascension alternation

The body-part possessor ascension alternation distinguishes verbs expressing CONTACT from all others. While I do not discuss CONTACT as a primitive relevant to the case of CEC property items its effect in the case of the body-part possessor alternation highlights the basic intuition underlying the concept of Change – i.e., the fact that this concept is one that is quite complex and expressed through a range of primitive notions and combinations of such primitives. Observe in the examples in (12) a separation between verbs such as *cut*, *touch* and *hit* as opposed to *break*:

(12) Restrictions on the body-part possessor ascension alternation (Levin 1993: 7)

  a. Margaret **cut** Bill's arm.
  b. Margaret **cut** Bill on the arm.
  c. Janet **broke** Bill's finger.
  d. *Janet **broke** Bill on the finger.
  e. Terry **touched** Bill's shoulder.
  f. Terry **touched** Bill on the shoulder.

g. Carla **hit** Bill's back.
h. Carla **hit** Bill on the back.

Note that items such as *cut, touch* and *hit* allow for a relationship of contact between an Agent (subject) and a body part to be expressed through use of the preposition *on*. The resultant alternation is not permitted in the case of a verb such as *break*. The difference observed between these items is the presence of the notion of CONTACT which is present in all verbs shown in (12) except *break*. Thus the notion of CONTACT appears to be one that is relevant in the context of the expression of Change.

In the section below I will look at the combination of MOTION + CONTACT in the conative alternation. I do this in the same spirit that I have looked at CONTACT here. Note that my intention is not to exhaustively decompose word meaning. Rather as it relates to CEC property items, the aim is to focus on what may be called primary (aspectual) primitives that point to the presence of Change in lexico-semantic representation. Along these lines, both CONTACT and MOTION as primitives will not be discussed beyond their involvement in transitivity alternations.

4.5.3 MOTION + CONTACT in the conative alternation

The conative alternation is one where a verb may be used in conjunction with the preposition *at* to express an attempted but not (necessarily) achieved action. This alternation highlights a distinction between verbs such as *cut* and *hit* as opposed to *break* and *touch*. The difference between these verbs lies in the fact that the former contain the combined meanings MOTION and CONTACT while the latter do not.

(13) Restrictions on the conative alternation (Levin 1993: 6, example 14)
 a. Margaret **cut** at the bread.
 b. Carla **hit** at the door.
 c. * Janet **broke** at the bread.
 d. * Terry **touched** at the cat.

As shown in these examples, the verbs *cut* and *hit* appear in the conative alternation where they are used to express an (attempted) action without an actual result. Essentially one part of the meaning composite (MOTION) is articulated but the other (CONTACT) is not established. This type of alternation is only available

to lexical items which contain both elements of meanings (MOTION and CON-
TACT). Thus items such as *break* (BECOME/CAUSE + BECOME) and *touch* (CONTACT)
do not permit this alternation since they do not contain both these elements of
meanings.

4.6 Observations

The complexity of Change is apparent in the way in which the presence or absence of particular elements of meaning determine the extent to which particular Non-stative verbs may be subject to transitivity alternations. This indicates that the notion of Change is decomposable. This is an important point that must be considered in relation to CEC property items expressing dual aspectual behaviour as the contrast between the Stative and Non-stative realisation of such items indicates the presence or introduction of specific primitives.

In relation to the general meaning components which serve to express different types of Change, it is useful to point out that while these have aspectual ramifications in that they define Change, they are not strictly speaking aspectual, whereas Change is. Thus, for example, we note that any expression of the feature Change, regardless of its exact composition, predisposes a predicate to a Telic (endpoint) interpretation, provided that the necessary semantic information is supplied in the internal argument or other constituents. In contrast, a [–Change] verb leaves a predicate Atelic regardless of the nature of the internal argument. Recall examples (1–2), repeated here for convenience:

(14)   a.   John **knows**. (Stative) (Atelic)

      b.   John **knows** the answer. (Stative) (Atelic)

      c.   John **knew** the answer. (Stative) (Atelic)

(15)   a.   John **runs**. (Non-stative) (Atelic)

      b.   John **runs** a mile. (Non-stative) (Telic)

      c.   John **ran** a mile (Non-stative) (Telic)

All instances of the verb *know* provide an Atelic interpretation while the interpretation associated with the Non-stative *run* varies between Telic and Atelic dependent on the nature of the internal argument. Such contrasts are consistently seen between Stative and Non-stative verbs. We note additionally that all the examples in (14) are Atelic although (14b) and (14c) contain internal arguments that may be regarded as finite[7] – fitting the aspectual feature requirement of the internal argument for Telicity. This is due to the fact that the Non-stative verb *run* in (14) contains the feature [+Change] while the Stative *know* in (15) is [–Change]. The pertinent aspectual difference between the verbs in these sentences is not the type of Change that they indicate but whether or not they indicate Change.

Nevertheless, it is a look at the different types of Change and the decomposability of this concept that has provided insights into the primitives that are involved. In particular, seminal works in the area of verb meaning reveal two types of Event Structures which express Change and one which does not. These are Transition and Process on one hand and State on the other. In the case of a Transition Event Structure, we have seen that this is characterised by primitives of Change such as CAUSE and BECOME consistent with its expression of a Change of state. While in the case of a Process Event Structure, the relevant element of meaning seems to be consistent with DO which conceptually separates Agency from Cause. A State Event Structure may be identified based on the absence of any element of meaning associated with Change.

In Chapter 5, I will provide an analysis of dual aspectual forms in CECs that makes use of the concept of Change, its decomposability and its presence at the level of Event Structure. We will see that primitives such as CAUSE, BECOME and DO may be called upon to account for the systematic Stativity/Non-stativity contrast that is observed in property items. Recall also, though, that these contrasts are not the same for all property items; hence, different classes will be distinguished and accounted for by appealing to differences in Event Structures and the morphological operations that may be performed on them.

It will become apparent that the existence of items displaying dual aspectual behaviour in CECs does not disprove the basic intuition that underlies the Stative/Non-stative distinction and inherent aspect despite arguments that have been made in Creole studies to this effect (cf. Jaganauth 1987).

---

[7]Verkuyl (1996) refers to the feature contributed by the internal argument as based on finiteness. This is similar to the feature "Specified Quantity of A" [SQA] that has been used in reference to the contribution of the verbal arguments to Telicity (see Tenny 1994; MacDonald 2008).

5 Towards a model for the classification of property items: Syntactic behaviour, event types and semantic interpretations

5.1 Background

In Chapter 3, I outlined the problem presented by dual aspectual forms in CECs. Assuming, as I do, that the verb makes a unique aspectual contribution to Aspect, we are faced here with the need for an explanation of the aspectual behaviour of these items in CECs. In essence, how do we account for the fact that a single lexical item can express different aspects if it is the case that each item is associated with a unique aspectual value? In Chapter 4, following Comrie's (1976) account of the Stative/Non-stative distinction, I identified the notion of Change as the distinguishing feature separating verbs that express Change from those that do not. Further to this, consistent with discussion of works such as that of Levin (1993), and the earlier works of McCawley (1968); Carter (1988); Dowty (1979); Pustejovsky (1988); Grimshaw (1990), I point to Change as a lexico-semantic concept indicated by primitive elements of meaning such as BECOME, CAUSE and DO.

The notion of Change as a semantic concept associated with some verbs and not with others is appealing in that it may, in the case of CECs, account for the default Tense interpretation of Stative versus Non-Stative verbs as recognised in the work of Bickerton (1975); Winford (1993); Gooden (2008) among others (see the discussion in Chapter 3). Nonetheless, as we have seen, this does not account for the case of CEC property items that may be conceived as expressing Change in some instances but not in others. The question is, if Change is a semantic feature of the verb, are items such as these both [+Change] and [−Change] at the same time or are they one or the other? These are the questions that authors on CECs such as Bickerton (1975); Jaganauth (1987); Winford (1993); Sidnell (2002) etc. have grappled with.

5 Syntactic behaviour, event types and semantic interpretations

In this chapter, I will focus on a categorisation of property items based on the aspectual behaviour that they display. This will result in an alternative classification to that presented by Winford (1993) which, as indicated in Chapter 3, is to my knowledge the most complete attempt at treating this group of items from the perspective of aspect. Winford (1993) approaches CEC property items along the lines of Dixon's (1977) semantic categories, positing a division between items expressing Physical Property as Non-stative and all others as Stative. According to him,

> Items expressing Physical Property behave rather like Change of state (process) verbs whose semantic features are compatible with Progressive aspect. Such verbs are essentially Non-stative. By contrast, it seems that items expressing the concepts associated with semantic types like Dimension, Colour, Human Propensity etc., behave rather like Stative verbs. (p. 187–188)

The basic intuition, that there are two different types of property items in terms of Stativity, is correct but it does not fully account for certain facts. In the first instance, Winford does not actually account for the fact that there are items across his semantic categories that display dual aspectual behaviour, i.e., appear in both Stative and Non-stative use. Nor does he address the semantics which allow for an item to be labeled Stative/Non-stative especially given the fact that some appear in dual aspectual use. And, in his attempt to treat property items across CECs, he does not account for the fact that there may be cross-linguistic variation in the aspectual behaviour of specific items. Recall as well that the members of his semantic classes do not all behave as predicted. In these regards, such a treatment may be said to be lacking in terms of both observational and explanatory adequacy.

Here, I will present a model for the analysis of property items in CECs based on syntactic and semantic criteria and the behaviour exhibited by JC items as discussed in Chapter 3. This model takes into consideration cross-linguistic variation that may be observed in the aspectual behaviour of lexical items. Such variation is attributable to the culturally based lexico-semantic conceptualisation of specific items, allowing for some to be treated as either State, Change of state or Process, depending on the pertinent language variety. Owing to the lexico-semantic differences that may exist, I will not attempt a general classification for specific lexical items across CECs as Winford does but will focus on Jamaican Creole (JC) for a classification – which may serve as a model for the classification of similar forms in other CECs.

I will show that there are two distinct classes of property items: The first is of the type *sik,* which appears as the Stative form 'sick', the inchoative 'get sick' and the transitive Non-stative 'make sick'. Items of this type will be classified as Class 1 items and identified based on their ability to express a Change of state from one (logical) opposition[1] to the next in their Non-stative use. Consistent with Pustejovsky (1988; 1991), I will argue that the members of this class have the Event Structure of Transition. The second group, Class 2, is the class of items that are inherently States; but several subclasses may be distinguished within this class. On one hand, there are items of the type *nyuu* 'new', *wotlis* 'worthless', *chupid* 'stupid' which are Stative items and do not vary in Stativity (Class 2a). On the other hand there are those items which are also essentially Stative but which I argue may be derived to express Non-stativity. In this latter use, they are characterised by the Event Structure of either Transition (Change of state) or Process. These include items such as JC *blak* 'black'/'become black'/'cause to become black'/, *red* 'red'/'become red'/'cause to become red'/(Class 2b[2]), vs. *jelas* 'jealous'/'behave jealously', *bad* 'bad'/'behave badly/misbehave' (Class 2c).

The chapter is organised as follows: In §5.2, I will outline the criteria for the categorisation of property items and a conceptual descriptive model based on Event Structure as introduced in Chapter 1 and further elaborated in Chapter 4. In §5.3, I will apply this model to a specific categorisation of property items in JC. I sum up my observations in §5.4.

5.2 Criteria for the categorisation of property items

5.2.1 Non-stative use: The progressive criterion

In the study of CECs as well as elsewhere, Vendler's (1967) Progressive criterion has been used to evaluate Stativity (see Jaganauth 1987; Bickerton 1975; Gooden 2008). The assumption generally is that the presence of Imperfective or Progressive aspect marking points to Non-stativity while its incompatibility with a predicate indicates that such a predicate is Stative. However, the well attested occurrence of Progressive aspect marking with verbs accepted as expressing Stativity (see Verkuyl 1996; Lyons 1977; Smith 1983; 1991, etc.) makes it difficult to accept the progressive criterion in and of itself as a reliable test for the inherent aspect

---

[1] This notion is elaborated in §5.2.3

[2] As we will see in my discussion in §5.3, items such as these in their use as colour references in JC may be somewhat resistant to this kind of Non-stative use. However where they appear Non-statively, they express a Change of state. They also appear in idiomatic uses with the meaning 'sooty' in the case of *blak* 'black' and 'burnt' in the case of *red.*

5 Syntactic behaviour, event types and semantic interpretations

of a verb. In Chapter 2, we saw that similar problems arise in the use of this criterion in the discussion of CECs (see §2.2.3).

In this case however, the progressive criterion allows for the evaluation of the type of Non-stative meaning that arises where Progressive aspect is allowed to interact with a predicate. Thus we note for example a difference in interpretation where Progressive aspect interacts with the verb *have* as opposed to *run* and *close* as shown below (Examples are recalled from Chapter 1, §1.3.1):

(1) (adapted from Lyons 1977: 707)

    a. She **has** a headache. (Stative)

    b. She **is having** a headache. (Non-stative)

    c. She **is having** one of her headaches. (Non-stative)

(2) John **is running**. (Non-stative)

(3)   a. The door is **closed**. (Stative)

    b. The door **is closing**. (Non-stative)

In (1), the presence of Progressive aspect with the Stative verb *have* enforces a viewpoint that is compatible with Non-stativity, namely a Processual viewpoint. Examples such as these have led authors such as Lyons (1977); Smith (1983) to pay attention to the meaning that arises in such instances rather than simply citing a restriction between Progressive aspect and a verb indicating Stativity. In particular, Lyons (1977) points to a restriction between Stative meaning and Progressive meaning (p. 707).

On a first examination of the examples in (1–3) it would appear that the Progressive serves the same purpose, namely it induces an ongoing Process interpretation. However, upon closer examination, there are differences in the interpretation of the verbs in (1), (2) and (3) as they interact with the Progressive. In the case of (1b–c) the use of the Progressive seems to extend the State *have a headache* by establishing a viewpoint of this situation as ongoing. Thus, both *having a headache* and *running* as in (2) may be taken to have occurred and in the context of the Progressive ongoing. However, in the case of the door *closing* (3b), this has not been achieved. In other words, *She is having a headache* entails that *She has a headache*. Also, *John is running* entails: *John ran*, however, *The door is closing* does not entail *the door has closed*.

Based on the interpretations that arise in the examples (1–3), it is apparent that while the presence of the Progressive is consistent with Non-stative interpretation, it is important to pay attention to the specific Non-stative interpretation

5.2 Criteria for the categorisation of property items

that arises in each case rather than the mere fact that this is possible. In the case of *run*, consistent with its status as a Process, with Progressive aspect it is interpreted as an ongoing Process. In the case of *close*, however, due to its status as Change of state item (Transition), what the use of the Progressive captures is a Change of state in progress.

Furthermore, in the case of *have* the Progressive viewpoint allows for its interpretation as an ongoing Process even though *have* in and of itself may be labelled a Stative predicate. In that case, the Progressive aspect rather than the inherent aspect of the verb may in this case be accredited with establishing a viewpoint where the verb *have* in *having a headache* is not interpreted as a State. Rather it is interpreted as a *series* of States – somewhat analogous to an ongoing Process. Guéron (2008) addresses this influence of the Progressive morpheme stating that,

> the ING morpheme which heads the particle in which the lexical vP is embedded "massifies" the spatial configuration vP denotes by multiplying its internal states. (p. 1822)

The approach articulated by Guéron seeks to account for the interaction between different elements in the composition of Aspect. Such an approach may be contrasted with the approach of Vendler (1967) which claimed a restriction in the occurrence of Progressive marking and verbs referring to States or Achievements. Lyons (1977) addresses this incompatibility of "stativity" and "progressivity" as explicable in terms of the "ontological distinction between static and dynamic situations" (p. 707). Within an analysis which takes into consideration the contribution of the different elements involved in Aspect, *have* as used here may be analysed as a State, a [−Change] verb interacting with the Progressive aspect – an interaction which results in an aspectual viewpoint that may be classified as Non-stative [+Change]. Despite the different interpretations associated with the use of *have* in (1) above, it may be analysed as a verb that is inherently associated with the value [−Change].

We will see for CECs that the presence of the Progressive (Imperfective) has more significance than just the indication of Non-stativity. In particular, I will argue in the case of items which appear in dual aspectual use that while some of these are inherently Non-stative and thus compatible with Non-stative meaning, others are morphologically derived to express Non-stativity. Of those that are derived, we will see that some are derived to express a Process and others a Change of state. The difference is not just based on the ability of these items to appear in Non-stative use but rather the subtle differences that are evident in their Non-stative interpretations.

5 Syntactic behaviour, event types and semantic interpretations

5.2.2 Non-stative use: Transitive alternation

Transitive alternation will be used here as a complement to the progressive criterion as a means of evaluating interpretations that arise in the Non-stative use of dual aspectual items. This alternation as a method for the evaluation of Non-stative meaning will only be applicable to forms which appear to vary with regard to whether or not they express an Agent or Cause. In Chapter 2 we saw that along with the interaction of items with Progressive aspect, work on dual aspectual forms in CECs also provided data where the introduction of an Agent or Cause allowed for Non-stative interpretation (see §2.2.5 in particular).

The verb *close* is a canonical example of an item that allows for this alternation in English as shown below (recall also the discussion of the causative/inchoative alternation in §4.5.1):

(4) (Pustejovsky 1991: 53)
   a. The door is **closed**.
   b. The door **closed**.
   c. John **closed** the door.

In these examples the item *closed* points to a State in (4a) with no reference to a Change of state; a Cause or Agent is not expressed or even implied. In (4b) the situation expressed is one which captures a Change of state with no indication of an Agent or Cause although one may be assumed. This illustrates the Inchoative use of *close*. However, (4c) is a clearly agentive usage where *John* is responsible for the Change of state resulting in the State of the door being closed. This illustrates the Causative use of *close*.

This alternation between the transitive and intransitive uses of a given form is particularly relevant for forms which may not be compatible with Progressive aspect but permit an alternation of this kind. Note for example that *sik* 'sick' in JC is only marginally acceptable in the Imperfective but is fully acceptable in transitive use. Compare:

(5) a. ?? Di   pikni a   sik.
         ART child ASP sick
         'The child is getting sick.'
     b. Di   fuud **sik** di   pikni.
         ART food sick ART child
         'The food sickened the child/caused the child to be ill.'

5.2 Criteria for the categorisation of property items

In similar cases where Imperfective (Progressive) aspect may not be immediately acceptable, the causative/inchoative alternation allows for an evaluation of the Non-stative interpretation.

Both the compatibility of an item with Imperfective aspect and its participation in the causative/inchoative alternation will be accepted in this work as tests as it regards the appearance of an item in Non-stative use. Additionally, the type of interpretation that arises once Non-stative expression is allowed will be considered. As noted in the case of *have* and *close*, there is a difference in interpretation of these items in Non-stative use which cannot be attributed to the different ways in which they appear in Non-stative use (i.e.: Progressive aspect and transitive variation). I will propose that the interpretation of an item in Non-stative use provides an indication of the inherent event type with which such an item is associated.

In the following, I will look at the different interpretations that may be associated with CEC property items in Non-stative use. In my evaluation I propose a link between these interpretations and the inherent event type with which they may be associated. It is based on this that I posit a possible categorisation of CEC property items in §5.3.

5.2.3 Event types and semantic interpretations: State, Transition and Process

In this section I will elaborate what may be seen as semantic criteria in the classification of CEC property items. It will become apparent that while a number of these items appear in Non-stative use, only some of these may be analysed as inherently Non-stative. In particular, we will see that there is justification for a general categorisation of this group of items as inherent Transition [+Change] as opposed to inherent State [−Change]. However, the identification of items which I evaluate as inherent States only *appearing* in Non-stative use provides a rationale for a sub-categorisation among State items yielding derived Transitions and derived Processes. I present the preliminaries of this analysis below.

As it regards the three primitive event types with which a verb may be lexically associated, recall that these are STATE, PROCESS, and TRANSITION (Pustejovsky 1988; 1991). A State is "an eventuality that is viewed or evaluated relative to no other event" while a Transition is a "single eventuality evaluated relative to another single eventuality" and a Process is "a sequence of identical eventualities" (Pustejovsky 1988: 22–23). These definitions when placed alongside the semantic behaviours observed for JC property items in §3.4 will illuminate criteria for my analysis of this group of items as constituting inherent Transitions on

5 Syntactic behaviour, event types and semantic interpretations

one hand and inherent States on the other. States may be further subdivided to include those that may be derived as either Transitions or Processes.

The different interpretations associated with JC property items in Non-stative use as discussed in §3.4 relative to the different event types with which an item may be associated form semantic criteria that I will discuss in this section. If we recall the discussion of property items in §3.4, we observed what appears on the surface to be three categories of items. Firstly those such *ded* 'dead' and also Colour items such *red* 'red' and 'black' which in Non-stative use indicate a Change of state. Secondly those of the type *chupid* 'stupid', *saaf* 'soft', *haad* 'hard' *swiit* 'sweet' etc. which do not appear in Non-stative use. The third group of items highlighted are those of the type *jelas* 'jealous' and *bad* 'bad' – these are distinguished from others which appear in Non-stative use in that they do not indicate a Change from one state to another but rather an ongoing Process.

A preliminary evaluation of the semantic behaviour displayed by property items relative to the three possible event types highlights two anomalies: The first is the case of items in Non-stative use which are consistent with Process. Based on the fact that such items appear in Stative use as well, it is reasonable to assume that they cannot be inherently associated with a Process event type. Taking as a premise that a State is more basic than a Process in terms of Event Structure (cf. Pustejovsky 1991, also Grimshaw 1990), the State use must be taken as reflecting the inherent status of items of this type and the Process use as derived. Also, it seems to be the case that the Process use of these items is less frequent and somewhat marginal across Creoles. It is based on this observation that I will analyse items which express a Process in their Non-stative use as inherently associated with the Event Structure State, and derived to express a Process.

The second anomaly that I observe is the case of items of the type *ded* 'dead' relative to Colour items such as *blak* 'black' and *red* 'red' in Non-stative use. They appear similar on the surface in that in Non-stative use, they all indicate a Change from one state to another. However, as I will argue below in §5.3, there is a subtle distinction between these groups of items which allows for the categorisation of one as INHERENT TRANSITIONS and the other as DERIVED TRANSITIONS. The distinction supplied is based on the notion of logical opposition. In my analysis, items of the type *ded* 'dead' in their Non-stative use are evaluated relative to a logical opposition of contrariety (DEAD:ALIVE) based on their Event Structure. Items of the type expressing Colour in Non-stative use are also evaluated relative to a logical opposition; however I note in this use that they express a logical opposition of contradiction as opposed to one of contrariety.

5.2 Criteria for the categorisation of property items

Where a logical opposition of contradiction exists, the relationship is between x and its negative counterpart NOT x (i.e.: BLACK:NOT BLACK). In such cases, Horn (1989), observes that this kind of negation

> cannot in general be read as opposition or contrariety: When we speak of the 'not great' [...] we do not pick out 'what is small' any more than 'what is of middle size', rather we refer simply to what is different from the great. (p. 5)

Based on this, I note a subtle distinction in the semantic behaviour of property items which express a Transition: Items of the type *ded* 'dead', *raip* 'ripe', *sik* 'sick', etc., in their Non-stative use, establish an opposition with their contraries whereby a Change of state is logically linked to 'alive', 'green' (lit. 'unripe'), and 'well', respectively. In the case of items expressing Colour on the other hand, a Change of state resulting in *blak* 'black' or *red* 'red' at best is linked to an opposition of NOT BLACK or NOT RED respectively, not to an opposition of contraries such as 'white' or 'green' for example. I assess this lack of specific information as associated with the fact that this Change of state meaning is not one that is inherently part of the Event Structure of such items but derived.

Based on these preliminary observations I will argue for a classification of CEC property items into Transitions and States. The class of State is further subdivided to account for derived Transitions and Processes. The basic identifying features involved in the classification are shown in (6):

(6) Criteria for the classification of CEC property items
  a. ability to appear in Non-stative use (Progressive/transitive)
  b. expression of a Change of state interpretation (in Non-stative use)
  c. type of logical opposition (contradiction vs. contrariety) in Non-stative use
  d. expression of a Processual (Activity) interpretation

Below in §5.3, I will apply these criteria to a classification of property items in JC.

5 Syntactic behaviour, event types and semantic interpretations

5.3 Property items in JC: Towards a classification

The distribution of the syntactic and semantic features in (6) will identify an item as a State, Transition, or derived Transition or Process. As the feature table (Table 5.1) shows, an item associated with a pure State Event Structure only is identified as lacking any of these features given the fact that it does not appear in Non-stative use. A Transition is positive for all features indicated and is identified through its association with the expression of an opposition of contrariety. A derived Transition is identified based on its expression of a logical opposition of contradiction in Non-stative use. A derived Process lacks the feature of a logical opposition and that of a Change of state (Table 5.1).

This model in Table 5.1 can be applied to all CECs to yield a descriptive classification of property items from a universal perspective of event types and their semantic connotations. However, the classification for specific lexical items may differ dependent on the lexico-semantic conceptualisation associated with such an item in a particular language or dialect as would be evidenced by its syntactic and semantic behaviour. In the sections below, I will apply the model above to JC for a specific categorisation of property items.

5.3.1 Transitions in JC

In Table 5.1, inherent Transitions are distinguished from all others, including derived Transitions based on the fact that they entail a logical opposition of contrariety. This type of opposition is taken to be inherent in that it provides explicit information on the original state involved previous to the Change of state in question. Consider the use of JC *raip* 'ripe' as shown below:

(7) a. Di   plantin ra**ip**.
        ART plantain ripe
        i. 'The plantain is ripe.'
        ii. 'The plantain ripened.'
    b. Di   plantin   a   ra**ip**.
        ART plantain ASP raip
        'The plantain is becoming ripe/ripening.'
    c. Di   igla   dem raip di   mango dem fi sel.
        ART vendor PL raip ART mango PL to sell
        'The vendors ripen the mangoes to sell (them).'

5.3 Property items in JC: Towards a classification

Table 5.1: A model for the classification of property items in CECs

Categories	Appear in Non-stative use (progressive/transitive variation)	Allow for CHANGE OF STATE interpretation	Encode PROCESSUAL INTERPRETATION	ENCODE LOGICAL OPPOSITION of Contrariety	ENCODE LOGICAL OPPOSITION of Contradiction
1. CHANGE OF STATE (Transition)[a]	✓	✓	✓	✓	✗
2A. STATE	✗	✗	✗	✗	✗
2B. STATE/DERIVED CHANGE OF STATE (Transition)	✓	✓	✓	✗	✓
2C. STATE/DERIVED PROCESS	✓	✗	✓	✗	✗

[a]There is a seeming absence of an account of the fact that items of this type appear also in Stative use. Given the general presumption that all property items appear in Stative use, my focus is on the question of their Non-stative appearances and their inherent aspectual status.

5 Syntactic behaviour, event types and semantic interpretations

Note here that *raip* 'ripe' appears in Stative use (7ai) and in clearly Non-stative uses in (7b) and (7c) which express in each case an overt Change of state. The Non-stative interpretation that is supplied in (7aii), shows as well that such an item in Stative use may be ambiguous between a "regular" State reading and a resultative reading. This as we will see, seems not to be the case for any Class 2 States.

What is characteristic of an item such as *raip* 'ripe' in JC is that in both its Stative and Non-stative interpretations, it may be said to be interpreted relative to a logical opposition which provides explicit information on its original state which is contrary to the State 'ripe'. In this case, in order for a Change of state to RIPE to take place; the understanding is that the original state of the item in question was logically GREEN (or 'unripe'). Thus, even for (7a) which expresses a State; this current State results from a processual Change of state from GREEN. In (7b–c), which express an explicit Change of state, the same is true, this results in a State. The Change of state is logically linked to an original State that starts out with the GREEN and the Change of state leads logically to a state of 'ripeness'. The difference in this case, however, is that the focus is on the Process which results in the State of 'ripeness' rather than the State itself (which has not yet been achieved).

There are a number of items in JC which may be shown to display behaviours similar to that of *raip* 'ripe'. Some of these are *kuul* 'cool', *hat* 'hot', *sik* 'sick', *wet* 'wet', etc. These all allow for Progressive aspect, transitive use and a Change of state interpretation which entails a logical opposition of contrariety:

(8) a. Di parij **kuul/ hat**.
 the porridge cool/hot
 i. 'The porridge is cool/hot.'
 ii. 'The porridge has cooled/has heated up.'

 b. Di parij a **kuul/hat**.
 the porridge ASP cool/hot
 'The porridge is cooling/heating (up).'

 c. Im **a kuul/hat** di parij.
 3SG ASP cool the porridge
 'He/She is cooling/heating the porridge.'

(9) a. Di kluoz dem **wet/jrai**.
 the clothes PL wet/dry
 i. 'The clothes are wet/dry.'
 ii. 'The clothes have become wet/dry.'

5.3 Property items in JC: Towards a classification

b. Di kluoz dem a wet/jrai pan di lain.
the clothes PL ASP wet/dry on the line
'The clothes are getting wet/drying on the line.'

c. Rien **wet** di kluoz dem pan di lain.
rain wet the clothes PL on the line
'Rain wet the clothes on the line.'

d. Son **jrai** di kluoz dem pan di lain.
sun dry the clothes PL on the line
'Sun dried the clothes on the line.'

(10) a. Di pikni **sik**.
the child sick
  i. 'The child is ill.'
  ii. 'The child became ill.'

b. ?? Di pikni **a sik**.[3]
the child ASP ill
'The child is getting ill.'

c. Di fuud **sik** di pikni.
the food sick the child
'The food made the child sick.'

As shown here, lexical items such as *kuul* 'cool', *hat* 'hot', *wet* 'wet', *sik* 'sick', etc. like *raip* 'ripe' appear in both Stative and Non-stative use. In the latter, they express a Change of state within a logical opposition between HOT:COLD, WET:DRY, and SICK:WELL, respectively.

Items of this type are those that are perhaps most suitably called dual aspectual forms: They may be said to inherently allow for both the Stative and Non-stative expressions as seen in the examples above. Nonetheless, items displaying such behaviour, although they appear in Stative and Non-stative use, are best seen as inherently Non-stative and associated with the abstract semantic feature [+Change]. This is based on the event type with which they are associated. Recall that the structure in Figure 5.1 captures the event type of Transition that is expressed by items of the type shown in examples (7–10).

Recall that a Transition is the merger of the notions Process and State where each is taken to be evaluated relative to the other. In other words, a lexical item

---

[3] This expression is marginally acceptable at best in JC. Hence, the compatibility of lexical items with Progressive aspect is not in and of itself a reliable test for (Non)-Stativity of an item.

5 Syntactic behaviour, event types and semantic interpretations

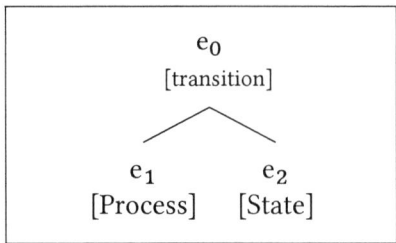

Figure 5.1: Transition Event Structure (Pustejovsky 1991: 56)

having the Event Structure of Transition, when expressing a State, is understood to entail a Process; when expressing a Process, a State is assumed as the endpoint.

Thus, upon a Stative interpretation (e_2), an item displaying the range of behaviour of JC *raip* 'ripe', *sik* 'sick', *kuul* 'cool', *hat* 'hot', *wet* 'wet', etc. must be understood relative to an opposition. Moreover, it must be understood in relation to the Process (e_1) that accounts for the culmination of the relevant State, although, in such a case, the (semantic) focus is on the State (e_2), i.e.: an attribute (result) rather than any Process that brought it about. This I believe distinguishes this kind of State interpretation from forms which are truly Stative, in that this Stativity is a resultative part of a larger template for a single word that is Non-stative whereas purely Stative forms do not share this same complex structure. While it may be argued that even in the case of Stative verbs there must have been a point at which that State was entered in, this is usually not a part of the meaning of the word itself and does not form a part of its Event Structure.

In previous studies in CECs, authors have been accustomed to analysing verbs purely in terms of an opposition between Stativity and Non-stativity (cf. Bickerton 1975; Jaganauth 1987; Winford 1993; Gooden 2008; etc). Based on Pustejovsky's identification of three distinct event types at this level, the basic opposition Stative/Non-stative may be applied to the Event Structure of State and Process respectively. However, the third Event Structure of Transition adds a complexity to this opposition in that it merges both concepts (State and Non-state) within one event type. This "merger" allows conceptually for two primitive event types determined by whether the focus is on the Process or on the resulting State within a Transition: What may be called a PROCESSUAL TRANSITION which focuses on a Process within the Transition and the resulting TRANSITIONAL STATE which focuses on the State within the Transition. The structure in Figure 5.2 is intended to capture this.

Figure 5.2 captures the shift in focus that a Transition Event Structure allows, where a speaker may choose to highlight the Stative or Non-stative aspect of a

5.3 Property items in JC: Towards a classification

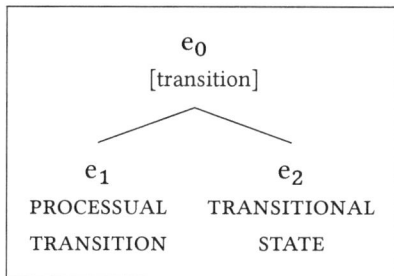

Figure 5.2: The two foci of the Transition Event Structure

situation. This type of choice is somewhat analogous to the choice that a speaker has as it regards viewpoint aspect where for example a verb indicating a State may be used in the context of Progressive viewpoint resulting in an overall Non-stative outlook (cf. Smith 1983).

The representation in Figure 5.2 reflects the fact that the Stative meaning (e_2) expressed within the context of a Transition is distinct from that of a pure State in that it entails a Change of state. Likewise the Non-stative meaning conceptually entails a resultant State and in this way is distinct from the Process associated with a Process Event Structure. Based on this, what we observe in the different uses of this class of dual aspectual forms is a shift in focus between a Processual Transition in the case of the Non-stative interpretation and a Transitional State in the case of the Stative interpretation. Both these are linked to a Transition Event Structure that is inherently Non-stative or [+Change].

5.3.2 States among JC property items

The second class of items based on the proposed model, are those which are States. This general group is diverse in that it contains items which may also be modified to express Non-stativity (Transition or Process). The most obvious items that would fit this class, however, are those which do not allow for Non-stative interpretation, the "pure" State items. This means that they are not compatible with Progressive aspect and do not participate in the transitive alternation. Examples of such items are shown below:

(11) a. Di siment **haad**.
 The cement hard
 'The cement is hard.'
 * 'The cement has hardened.'

5 *Syntactic behaviour, event types and semantic interpretations*

    b. *Di siment a **haad**.
        the cement ASP hard
        'The cement is hardening.'

    c. *Dem **haad** di siment.
        3PL hard the cement
        'They made the cement hard.'

(12) a. Di lemanied **swiit**.
        the lemonade sweet
        'The lemonade is sweet.'
        * 'The lemonade has been sweetened.'

    b. *Di lemanied a **swiit**.
        the lemonade ASP sweet
        'The lemonade is getting sweet.'

    c. *Dem **swiit** di lemanied.
        3SG sweet the lemonade
        'They sweetened the lemonade/made the lemonade sweet.'

(13) a. Da man de **chupid**.
        that man LOC stupid
        'That man is stupid.'
        * 'That man has become stupid.'

    b. *Da man de a **chupid**.
        that man LOC ASP stupid
        'That man is getting/behaving stupid.'

    c. *Di uman **chupid** di man.
        the woman stupid the man
        'The woman made the man stupid.'

(14) a. Di riva **waid/lang/braad**,
        ART river wide/long/broad
        'The river is wide/long/broad,'
        'The river has been widened/lengthened/broadened.'

    b. di riva a **waid/lang/braad**,
        ART river ASP wide/long/broad
        'The river is widening/lengthening/broadening.'

5.3 Property items in JC: Towards a classification

 c. *Dem a **waid/lang/braad** di riva.
  3PL ASP wide/long/broad ART river
  'They are widening/lengthening/broadening/the river.'

As shown here, there is a clear group of items in JC which are restricted in their ability to appear in Non-stative use. Examples such as *haad* 'hard', *swiit* 'sweet', *chupid* 'stupid', *waid* 'wide', *lang* 'long' and *braad* 'broad' are used in the examples above to show this restriction.

Items which display this type of behaviour are classified here as State consistent with the Event Structure in Figure 5.3.

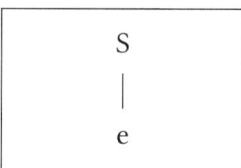

Figure 5.3: State Event Structure (Pustejovsky 1991: 56)

Recall that the structure in Figure 5.3 represents an event type that is not viewed or evaluated relative to any other event. What this means essentially is that the item behaves the way it does because of how it is conceived by the speaker or the community. Thus it may be said that in JC, items such as *haad* 'hard', *swiit* 'sweet', *chupid* 'stupid', *waid* 'wide', *lang* 'long' and *braad* 'broad' are not conceived as inherently involving a Change of state and are not open to the introduction of an external Cause or Agent.

In reality however, it must be noted that there may be a degree of flexibility in the behaviour of an item across Creoles, or across dialects within a Creole and even among individual speakers. Thus the thrust should be towards a behavioural model which accounts for the fact that an item is able to behave the way it does. A case in point is the behaviour of *braad* 'broad'. The cognate item *bradi* in Sranan appears in both Stative and Non-stative use as seen in §3.4. Likewise, there is a possible classification for JC that would include *braad* in a different category to that indicated above. Consider (15) for example

(15) JC
  Mi a waak chuu di duor wid di bag eng dong pan mi
  1SG ASP walk through ART door with ART bag hang down on 1SG
  shuolda an mi beli a **braad**.
  shoulder and 1SG belly ASP broad
  'I am walking through the door with the bag hanging on my shoulder and

my belly broadening out (looking broad).'

This sentence was produced[4] by a JC speaker from St. Elizabeth within the following context: She arrives at work and, entering through the door which has a mirror, she catches a glimpse of herself in the mirror. What I listed as a property item with an Event Structure of (pure) State – an Event Structure which does not allow for Non-stative expression, in this case appears in Non-stative use. The meaning indicated here suggests that at least for this speaker, JC *braad* 'broad' may be conceived as a Transition or a State of the type that is open to the introduction of an external Cause or Agent, in other words a State which may be derived as a Transition or a Process. The distinction here would depend on whether the perspective given is one where the bag was responsible for the 'broadening' of her belly (Cause) or whether her belly just appeared broad as she walked. This is nonetheless an interesting use of the Progressive aspect to express a viewpoint and would deserve further examination in a precise classification for this variety of JC.

The point made here is that any actual classification of particular lexical items must be flexible enough to allow for the variation that is evident in this group of items. Also, a model in this regard should have the tools to account for why it is that an item is able to behave the way it does. In this instance, it appears that while a lexical item such as *braad* in one variety of JC may be a State and not open to the introduction of Non-stative elements of meanings, in another variety, it may allow for derivation into a Transition. Ultimately, a classification of an item must take as its point of departure its specific behaviour within the context of the variety under study in relation to the syntactic and semantic criteria outlined in Table 5.1.

In the sections below, I will look at State items in Non-stative use.

5.3.3 On the Non-stative use of State items

5.3.3.1 Derived Transitions

A closer look at the group of items which may be classified as States shows that there are also those which, in contrast to items (11–14) allow for Non-stative use. Consider first items denoting Colour such as *red* 'red' and *blak* 'black':

(16) a. Di shuuz **blak**.
 ART shoes black
 'The shoe is black.'

---

[4]February 23, 2010.

5.3 Property items in JC: Towards a classification

b. ?? Di shuuz a **blak/red**.
   ART shoes ASP black
   'The shoe is getting black.'

c. ?? Dem **blak/red** di shuuz.
   3PL black/red ART shoes
   'They are making the shoe black/blackening the shoe.'

Items expressing Colour such as *red* 'red' and 'black' as shown here, in Non-stative use would only be marginally accepted in JC. However, there are cases where these items may be shown to be acceptable in Non-Stative use. Consider the examples (17–19) for example:

(17) im **red** im 'an dem wid jragan blood
     3SG red 3SG hand PL with dragon blood
     'He used dragon blood[5] to redden his hand.'

(18) a. Di mango dem **red**.
        ART mango PL red
        'The mangoes are red.'

     b. Di mango dem **red** pan di chrii.
        ART mango PL red on ART tree
        'The mangoes got red on the tree.'

     c. Di son **red** di mango dem pan di chrii.
        ART sun red ART mango PL on ART tree
        'The sun reddened the mango.'

(19) a. Di doti gyas **blak** di pat dem.
        ART dirty gas black ART pot PL
        'The dirty gas made the pot black/sooty.'

     b. Chuu di gyas doti di pat dem a **blak**.
        because ART gas dirty ART pot PL ASP black
        'The pots are getting black/sooty because of the dirty gas.' (that is used for cooking)

In the examples, (16–19) the items *red* 'red' and *blak* 'black' in Non-stative use, express what I analyse as the Event structure of a derived Transition. Similar

---

[5]Note that 'dragon blood' is a plant whose leaves when rubbed together produce a red substance that may be used as a kind of dye.

to the semantic interpretation associated with Transitions, in (16), the marginal Non-stative use of *red* 'red' and *blak* 'black', denotes a Change of state. I treat this as derived based on the fact that they do not in their Non-stative use establish the same type of logical opposition as inherent Transitions which I associate with an opposition of contraries. Thus, where JC RIPE:UNRIPE or MAD:SANE, express a logical opposition where a particular state is implied as the original state of the item, in the Non-stative use of an item such as *blak* 'black', this is not so. Essentially, there is no implication about the initial state of the item; in (16) for example, the *shuuz* may have been white, purple, blue or faded black etc. The introduction of elements of meanings such as BECOME and CAUSE allow for the Change of state interpretation that is apparent in (16b–c) but these are not linked in an opposition of contrariety.

The marginal Non-stative use of these items as shown in (16) would not be enough to provide a basis for a class of derived Transitions among JC property items. However, the acceptability of the Non-stative use of these colour terms in (17–19) indicates a need for an account that extends beyond the Stative appearance of these items to account for the fact that they may also appear in Non-stative use. The notion of a derived Event Structure is an attempt to capture and account for such a usage. Note however, that there are differences in the meanings that are expressed in the Non-stative use of these colour terms. In (17), the use of the item *red* 'red' is clearly related to the colour term, but (18) and (19) may be analysed as idiomatic uses (i.e.: not as regular Colour denoting term). In (18a–b) it is used to refer to the Change of state which results from the sun causing the mangoes to appear *red* 'red' through burning thereby establishing an opposition between 'burnt' and 'not burnt'. Similarly *blak* 'black' in (19) is used to express a Change of state resulting in 'sooty'.

The idiomatic uses these items seem to suggest the possibility of lexical items different from the colour terms themselves and thus a different categorization altogether, possibly that of inherent Transition. The behaviour of these items in this regard would merit further investigation. Nevertheless, I would like to point out even in these idiomatic uses, what appears to be a clear association with the Colour terms *red* 'red' and *blak* 'black': The burning of the mango physically results in the colour *red*. Likewise, although 'sooty' represents a special kind of *black* that is arrived at through burning and smoke, the physical result is the colour black. Note as well that the usage of *red* 'red' in (17) reflects one that is not idiomatic.

Based on these observations, I am inclined to maintain a categorisation of these as derived Transitions within the group of States among property items in JC.

5.3 Property items in JC: Towards a classification

Beyond JC as well, work by Alleyne (1987) shows items of this type (expressing colour) occurring in Non-stative use for Sranan suggesting that such a Class is relevant to CECs as well.

The examples in (16–19) seem to establish a contrast with those items shown in (11–14). However, despite the seeming separation between such forms based on syntactic criteria, I would like to suggest that these are unified as inherently associated with an Event Structure of State. In order to account for the ability of the items in (16–19) to appear in Non-stative use, I posit that these are open to a morphological process which introduces Non-stative elements of meanings into their Event Structure. This is consistent with the representation of Carter (1988) (discussed in Chapter 4) which shows a relationship between DARK:DARKEN.

In analysing the Non-stative use of such items I would like to propose that their Event Structure is one that is similar to that of a Transition. However, as shown in Figure 5.4, the Change of state aspect is derived through the addition of another Event Structure level.

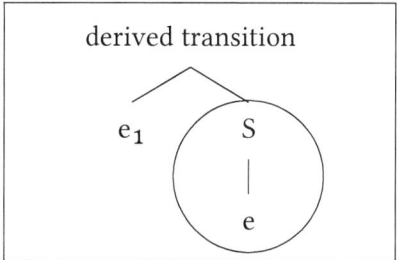

Figure 5.4: An Event Structure representing derived Transition

Note here that a State (S) Event Structure as represented by Pustejovsky (1991) forms the base of this structure. This is merged with the Event Structure representation of Transition to show the introduction of Non-stative elements of meanings, namely those that are associated with a first sub-event (e_1) that would result in a State. What I propose is that the Non-stative version of an item such as *blak* 'black' arises through a covert morphological process that affects the Event Structure of the State item *blak* 'black' allowing for the expression of a Transition. In this way *blak* 'black' is able to express a Change from one State to another; however, this Change of state initiated by e_1 is not inherently linked to the logical contrary of BLACK which is WHITE.

Two Non-stative possibilities are evident based on the examples in (16): The inchoative version (16b) which shows the *shuuz* 'shoe(s)' as the affected entity (Theme) in subject position and the transitive version which shows a Cause or

Agent in the position of subject (16c). In the case of the inchoative version, it may be posited that a semantic primitive BECOME is covertly introduced into the representation of the lexical item that accounts for this expression. The primitive BECOME is directly related to the Theme argument of the State, thus there is no change in the syntactic structure.

However in the case of the transitive version (16c), it is a CAUSE primitive that may be said to account for the change in the syntactic structure, namely the introduction of a Cause/Agent and the transitivity that contrasts with the Stative version in (16a). Regarding this, consistent with the implications of the structure in Figure 5.4, Grimshaw (1990) observes that a Cause argument will be associated with the "first sub-event which is causally related to the second sub-event" (p. 26). Thus, the introduction of the primitive CAUSE accounts for the change in transitivity that is seen in (16c) as opposed to (16a).

In §5.3.3.2, I will look at the case of derived Process as they appear in JC.

5.3.3.2 Derived Processes

There is a second group of items among States which, like the State items discussed above appears in Non-stative use. However, in Non-stative use such items are consistent with a Process Event Structure. Examples of these are shown in (20) and (21):

(20) a. Dat de pikni **bad/ruud**!
 that FOC child bad/rude
 'That child is a bad/rude child!'

 b. Dat de pikni a **bad/ruud** lang taim.
 that FOC child ASP bad/rude long time
 'That child has been misbehaving for a long time.'

(21) a. Dem **jelas**.
 3PL jealous
 'They are jealous.'

 b. Dem a **jelas** mi fi di kyar we mi jraiv.
 3PL ASP jealous 1SG for ART car that 1SG drive
 'They are (being) jealous/envious of me because of my car.'

In these examples, items such as *bad* 'bad', *ruud* 'rude' and *jelas* 'jealous', which appear in Stative use, also appear in Non-stative use. In contrast to those items denoting colour, they provide an interpretation that is consistent with a Process. The difference between these and standard Processes such as *run, push*, etc. is that the latter do not appear in Stative use.

I analyse items displaying this behaviour as inherent States derived to express a Process Event Structure. This is based on the primacy of State (Grimshaw 1990) and the fact that inherent Processes do not also express States. In these derived Processual uses, I associate such items with an Event Structure of Process as shown in Figure 5.5.

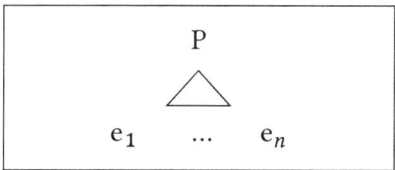

Figure 5.5: Event Structure of Process (Pustejovsky 1991: 56)

In contrast to the "eventuality that is viewed or evaluated relative to no other event" in the (a) examples, the examples in (b) are more consistent with a "sequence of identical eventualities" (Pustejovsky 1988: 22).

5.4 A classification of property items in JC

Based on the examination of JC, the classification in Table 5.2 may be posited. The classification in Table 5.2 represents a behaviour-based model which classifies a lexical item in accordance with its semantic and syntactic behaviour. Note that this categorisation that I posit may vary from that which may be observed for other authors dependent on the variety of JC that is under study. For example, Bailey (1966) points to the occurrence of an item such as *fat* with Progressive aspect (cf.: *Im a fat* 'S/He's getting fat', p. 47). What this indicates is variation in the categorisation of fat dependent on the variety of JC under study. Similarly, in the case of *braad* 'broad' as we saw in (15), the different behaviours associated with a particular item may warrant a different categorisation based on the specific variety under study.

The model in Table 5.2 is designed to accommodate the variability that has been observed in the behaviour of this group of items. In this regard, it may be taken to replace that of Winford (1993), which as discussed in Chapter 3, fails to capture the variability in behaviour that exists across semantic categories. Note for example here that the group of Transitions for JC includes items from the

5 Syntactic behaviour, event types and semantic interpretations

Table 5.2: A classification for property items in JC

Categories	JC items	Appear in Non-stative use[a]	Allow for CHANGE OF STATE[b]	Encode PROCESSUAL interpretation	Encode a logical opposition	
					CONTRARIETY	CONTRADICTION
1. CHANGE OF STATE[c]	mad, wet, kuul, raip, sik, hat ded drai, ful sik	✓	✓	✓	✓	✗
2a. STATE	saaf, haad, chupid wotlis, sowa nyuu, oul, big, fain, fat, maawga, braad, etc.	✗	✗	✗	✗	✗
2b. DERIVED CHANGE OF STATE[d]	blak, red	✓	✓	✓	✗	✓
2c. DERIVED Activity	jelas, bad, ruud, etc.	✓	✗	✓	✗	✗

[a] Progressive/transitive variation
[b] (NON-STATIVE) interpretation
[c] Transition
[d] Transition

semantic categories of Human Propensity (*mad*), along with those classified as expressing Physical Property. Similarly, the State items are a mix of those expressing Physical Property, Dimension and Age. In this way, the actual behaviour of an item is captured in its classification.

The analysis that I propose here, although based on earlier semantic-based works such as that of Carter (1988); McCawley (1968); Dowty (1979); Pustejovsky (1988; 1991) and Grimshaw (1990), is also compatible with syntax-based approaches such as that articulated in Larson (1988), and Travis (2010). In particular, regarding Larson's VP shell analysis, it may be noted that a VP shell is associated with each primitive element that is included in the proposed analysis. This accounts, for example, for the fact that; the introduction of CAUSE at the level of primitive Event Structure, translates to a corresponding Cause argument at the level of vP. Similarly the introduction of DO at the level of Event Structure means the introduction of an Agent argument at the syntactic level of vP. This is consistent with the distinct differences observed between clearly Stative and Non-stative versions of dual aspectual items.

5.5 Summary

What we have seen in this analysis of dual aspectual forms may be summarised as a general descriptive approach to this category of items in CECs captured in the following questions:

(22) a. Does a particular item allow for both Stative and Non-stative interpretation? (All Class 1 items do, class 2 is divided)
b. In the Non-stative variation, is there an inherent opposition between contraries i.e.: is specific information implied on the initial state of the item in question? This separates items that I have labelled as Class 1 items from those Class 2 items that may be morphologically derived into Change of state predicates (2b).
c. Is the Non-stative interpretation one that includes Change through Agency but does not include a Change of state? This separates items of Class 2b from 2c.

The treatment that I propose here for dual aspectual forms addresses the class of property items in CECs as diverse, based on their semantic and syntactic behaviours. From the perspective of an Event Structure analysis, items within this general group are evaluated and classified consistent with the notions of Transition, Process and State. In this way, they are associated with a unique aspectual value in accordance with their Event Structure. The notion of a Transition Event Structure and the introduction of meaning components consistent with the expression of Change accounts for the duality in aspectual expression that we see in those items which appear in both Stative and Non-stative use. This treatment effectively separates inherently dual aspectual forms from other items which are either purely Processual or Stative in character.

This analysis is not restricted to a particular (Creole) language but may be applied to a treatment of property items generally. Since it is expected that different language communities will have different conceptualisations associated with particular items, the actual categorisation of items may differ across speech communities. Nevertheless, general behavioural patterns consistent with event types will be observed allowing in each case for language specific generalisations over sets of items. In the following chapter I will analyse the implications that such an analysis has for the categorial status of property items.

6 Summing up: On the categorial status of dual aspectual forms – The implications of an aspectual analysis of CEC property items

6.1 Overview

In this study, I have focused on the question of the unique contribution of the verb to Aspect in CECs and argued in this regard that the verb makes a unique contribution to Aspect in the form of the Stative/Non-stative distinction and the feature [Change]. The question of the aspectual contribution of the verb in CECs is closely tied to the observation in the study of Tense in CECs, that the interpretation of the unmarked verb differs dependent on the type of verb involved (Stative/Non-stative). In this regard, Bickerton (1975) notes that the default interpretation of unmarked Statives is Present while that of Unmarked Non-stative is Past. Such a position which holds the Stative/Non-stative distinction as relevant in Tense-Aspect interpretation is intuitively appealing but it has nonetheless been fraught with problems in Creole studies.

As indicated (Chapter 2), there have been numerous counterexamples to Bickerton's claims regarding the Stative/Non-stative distinction. First, the restriction on the occurrence of Progressive aspect marking with Stative verbs has been shown to be problematic. Second, the Tense interpretations that he predicts for Stative as opposed to Non-stative verbs have been shown to be variable, dependent on context and other factors. However, authors such as Winford (1993), and Gooden (2008) have provided some support for Bickerton's observations but point to the Stative/Non-stative distinction as "only a part of the story" (Gooden 2008: 307). Both these authors indicate that the influence of other factors such as adverbials and context may account for anomalous interpretations. In this regard, Gooden (2008) points out that "in many cases discourse has been shown to be relevant in precisely those cases in which Bickertonian formulation of "aspect" fails" (p. 307–308). This being the case, much more than the issue of the

6 Summing up: On the categorial status of dual aspectual forms

observational adequacy of the Stative/Non-stative distinction is its explanatory adequacy. The matter of items which appear in both Stative and Non-stative use (dual aspectual items) in CECs raises this question. For this reason, items of this type have been the primary area of concern in this study.

In addressing the question of the unique contribution of the verb to Aspect, I identified the basic Event Structure with which a lexical item is associated as the mechanism by which an item may be labelled as either [+Change], i.e.: a Transition or Process, or [−Change], i.e.: a State (Pustejovsky 1988; 1991). In accounting for dual aspectual forms I looked at these items as forming part of the general group of property items in CECs and proposed a classification of this group of items based on the aspectual behaviour they display. My findings in this area revealed two distinct classes of items: Those that are inherent Transitions and associated with the feature [+Change] and those that are inherent States and associated with the feature [−Change]. Note that there are no dual aspectual forms which are inherent Processes.

The categorisation that I propose is not just based on the syntactic behaviour of these items (i.e.: their ability to appear in Non-stative use) but also on the semantic behaviours that they display in Non-stative use. Thus I note a clear group of items which appear in Non-stative use and are inherently Non-stative (Class 1: JC *raip* 'ripe', *wet* 'wet', *sik* 'sick', *ded* 'dead', *jrai* 'dry', etc.) and likewise a group of items which never appear in Non-stative use and are consequently Stative (Class 2a: JC: *saaf* 'soft', *haad* 'hard', *chupid* 'stupid', *oul* 'old', *fat* 'fat', etc.). However, the crucial point is the identification of two groups of items that appear in Non-stative use but which in my analysis are inherently Stative (Class 2b: JC *red* 'red' and *blak* 'black' 2c: JC *jelas* 'jealous', *bad* 'bad', *ruud* 'rude', etc.). The recognition of these as separate classes is based on the semantic interpretations with which they are associated in Non-stative use.

Items such as JC *jelas* 'jealous' and *bad* 'bad' when evaluated in Non-stative use, express a Process. Thus, I analysed these as morphologically derived to express this Event Structure. The colour terms *red* 'red', and *blak* 'black' where they appear in Non-stative use express a Change of state (Transition). This particular class merits further investigations based on the idiomatic uses that may be associated with them in Non-stative use. Nevertheless I have argued for these as a class of derived Transitions as there is evidence of clearly acceptable non-idiomatic uses.

The notion of logical opposition and the distinction between an opposition of contrariety and an opposition of contradiction was critical in identifying the difference between those items which are inherent Transitions and those which are derived. As I showed in Chapter 5, items that are Transitions express a Change of state from one state to another. Consistent with their Event Structure, these are evaluated relative to their logical opposite. The difference between inherent and derived Transitions as I observed was that inherent Transitions such as, *ded* 'dead', *jrai* 'dry' *raip* 'ripe', *sik* 'sick', etc. were evaluated relative to an opposition that explicitly points to the original state of the items in question. Thus a Change of state resulting in *ded* 'dead' implies an original state of ALIVE, similarly for *jrai* 'dry' – WET, *raip* 'ripe' – GREEN and, *sik* 'sick' – WELL, etc. These oppositions are consistent with a relationship of contrariety. But derived Transitions establish a different kind of opposition in that they do not specify explicitly an original state for the items in question but rather what they were not. Thus, items expressing Colour, where permitted to appear in Non-stative use, are interpreted as the result of a Change of state process from a previous state that was for example 'not RED' or 'not BLACK'. The opposition indicated by these is that of contradiction as there is no clear commitment to the original state of the items in question.

This analysis which provides an explanation of the behaviour of these items points to a sound basis for the Stative/Non-stative distinction at the level of primitive Event Structure. Thus Bickerton's observation of the centrality of the Stative/Non-stative distinction in Creole studies is validated. Even more than this, however, the study feeds into the longstanding debate on the categorial status of items of this type as either verbs or adjectives. The analysis which I have proposed indicates a group of items that are diverse in terms of their aspectual status comprising those that are inherently Non-stative and those that are inherently Stative. This analysis, when extended to a discussion of the categorial status of these items, points to diversity in the category of these items as well – a difference in this work when compared to others which have attempted to treat property items as a unified group.

In summing up in this chapter, I look specifically at the implications that the analysis that I have presented has for the discussion of the categorial status of the items in question. I will focus on this in §6.2 and conclude in §6.3 by looking at the contribution of this work to scholarship and scope for further study.

6.2 On the categorial status of dual aspectual forms

With regards to the categorial status of property items in CECs, my study points to a diverse group of items constituting verbs, adjectives and derived verbs and adjectives. Taking as a basic assumption that diverse aspectual status translates to diverse categorial status, what we see is Class 1 items as (Non-stative) verbs;

these allow for derived adjectival use in their Stative appearances. In the case of Class 2 items, these are analysed as (Stative) adjectives with some allowing for derivation as verbs. This analysis is distinct from that of previous authors who, as seen in Chapter 3, have attempted to treat this group of items as a monolithic group of either (Stative) verbs or adjectives. The diversity of categorial status that I posit, captures the diversity in the actual behaviour that can be observed for these items. This is consistent with the observation of Kouwenberg (1996) who states that "taking adjectivals as a single class of lexical items seems to be a misguided approach" (p. 8). Note however that even while positing a diversity in aspectual and categorial status, at no point do I consider these forms to be Stative verbs in JC- or other CECs, excepting perhaps the Suriname Creoles.

In the sections below, I will deal with each Class of items that was identified in this study from the perspective of their categorial status. As will be seen, my concern is not with whether these items are able to appear in both adjectival and verbal use – that they appear in these uses is generally accepted in the literature. I will take prima facie the appearance of a property item in Non-stative use as the instantiation of a (Non-stative) verb. Likewise, I will take the appearance of a property item in Stative use as an instantiation of an adjective. My intention, as it was in the analysis of the aspectual status of these items, will be to provide an account of why it is that these items can appear in such uses. I look at each Class of items in turn.

6.2.1 Class 1 property items as Non-stative verbs

Class 1 property items are those which, as indicated in Chapter 5, not only allow for both Stative and Non-stative expressions but in Non-stative use show a Change of state within a logical opposition of contrariety. The example in (1) below, which features the JC item *wet/jrai* 'wet/dry' recalls example (9) from Chapter 5 for ease of reference:

(1)   a.   Di   kluoz   dem **wet/jrai**.
           ART clothes PL   wet/dry
             i.   'The clothes are wet/dry.'
             ii.   'The clothes have become wet/dry.'
        b.   Di   kluoz   dem   a   **wet/jrai** pan di   lain.
           ART clothes PL   ASP wet/dry on   ART line
           'The clothes are drying/getting wet on the line.'

6.2 On the categorial status of dual aspectual forms

c. Rien **wet** di kluoz dem pan di lain.
rain wet ART clothes PL on ART line
'Rain wet the clothes on the line.'

d. Son **jrai** di kluoz dem pan di lain.
sun dry ART clothes PL on ART line
'Sun dried the clothes on the line.'

As seen here, items such as *wet* 'wet' and *jrai* 'dry' may express a State as shown in (1a) but may also point overtly to a Change of state in (1b–d). Crucially however, (1a–d) all entail a logical change from one State to another. This is seen in the contrary opposition denoted by DRY and WET. This Change of state within a logical opposition of contrariety essentially is the distinctive characteristic of Class 1 (Transition) property items.

Further to the semantic behaviour of an item such as *jrai* 'dry', we note also its distribution where it is preceded by the aspectual marker *a* in (1c) as opposed to (1a) where it appears unmarked. So far in this work, the mere ability of an item to appear with the Imperfective aspect marker has not held any significance outside of its function in creating a context for the evaluation of Non-stativity. In this sense, both (1c) and (1d) have the same significance and the possibility of either one of these syntactic realisations would be sufficient for the purposes of this study. However, as is evident from the discussion of works such as Winford (1993); Sebba (1986); Seuren (1986) also Kouwenberg (1996), the syntactic behaviour of items such as *jrai* 'dry' has been a central factor in addressing their categorial status: The acceptability of Imperfective aspect and the possibility of transitive use provide evidence of verb status (see Chapter 3).

In my analysis, I take into consideration the mechanism that allows a form such as *jrai* 'dry' to display the type of syntactic and semantic behaviour that it does as opposed to other items which are more restricted (see §6.2.2 below). This lies in the conceptual structures of these items and the event type that is associated with them. In §5.3.1, where I discussed items displaying syntactic and semantic behaviours similar to that shown by *wet* 'wet', and *jrai* 'dry' in (1), I discussed these as associated with an Event Structure of Transition. I argued that a logical implication of this is the ability of these items to express both Stativity and Non-stativity consistent with adjectival and verbal uses, respectively. This is related to the structure of the event frame associated with these items which in one instance may allow for a resultative type focus (State/adjective) and in another for a focus on the Change of state (Process/verbal) meaning involved. Figure 5.1 from Chapter 5 is recalled here as Figure 6.1 for convenience.

6 Summing up: On the categorial status of dual aspectual forms

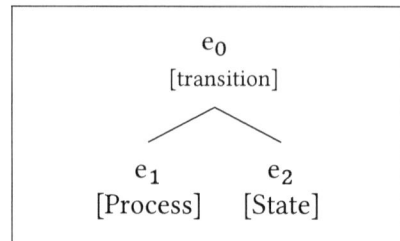

Figure 6.1: Transition Event Structure (Pustejovsky 1991: 56)

A Transition Event Structure, as previously discussed (§5.3.1), encompasses both a State meaning and a Process meaning. These different appearances that are observed for an item such as *jrai* 'dry' may be linked to a unique classification of items of this type as (Non-stative) verbs. This is consistent with my analysis of such items as linked to a unique Event Structure that is [+Change] even though they may be used both Statively and Non-statively. In these regards, I acknowledge the instantiation of *jrai* 'dry' above in (1a) as an adjective or verb dependent on its focus: In the case of (1ai) the focus is on the State (e_2) and adjectival while in (1aii) the focus is on the Process (e_1) and verbal. From the perspective however, of syntactic use as linked to an abstract lexico-semantic specification, both the verbal and adjectival use may be associated with a unique specification of such items as verbal and Non-stative at the conceptual level.

Note that this analysis explains the ambiguity of interpretation that is evident in the (a) examples. While Stative meaning does not always translate into adjectival status (cf.: SM *satu* 'to be salt' in Kouwenberg 1996) the behaviour of items such as 'wet' and 'dry' in JC, point to these as derived adjectives. This is consistent with the ambiguous interpretations indicated for (2) below:

(2)   a.   di   **jrai** kluoz   dem
              ART dry clothes PL

          i. 'the dry clothes'

          ii. 'the dried clothes'

      b.   di   kluoz   dem we   **jrai**
              ART clothes PL   what dry

          i. 'the clothes that are dry'

          ii. 'the clothes that are dried'

The suggestion of a Process that is evident in the ambiguous Stative interpretations that are shown here, provides an argument for the status of such items

6.2 On the categorial status of dual aspectual forms

in Stative use as derived adjectives (cf. Kouwenberg 1996).

Pustejovsky's (1991) representation of a Transition Event Structure may be modified to reflect this analysis of items in this class from the perspective of their categorial status (Figure 6.2).

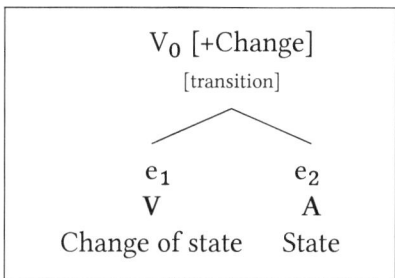

Figure 6.2: Transition Event Structure as reflecting a Change of state verb

As shown here, an abstract verb with the Event Structure of Transition may be realised as either a verb or adjective dependent on whether the syntactic focus is on the Change of state (e_1) it encodes or the result brought about by this Change of state (e_2). Based on the inherent [+Change] verbal status that is associated with this Event Structure, the adjectival uses of items associated with this event type must be analysed as derived. Items reflecting the behaviour of JC 'wet' and 'dry' may thus be analysed as inherently associated with a [+Change] verbal status and derived in its appearance as an adjective.

This analysis on some level may seem counter intuitive for authors who have been focused mainly on the syntactic appearance of such items (whether verbal or adjectival). Nonetheless, it is appealing from several angles. Firstly, from the perspective of the link between the semantic and syntactic levels; this approach establishes a connection between these two areas where a particular primitive Event Structure has consequences for the syntactic behaviour that a lexical item may display. Secondly, we are able to explain the different realisations of property items as both verbs or adjectives, and the semantic link between these realisations. In the case of items displaying the behaviour of *jrai* 'dry' their Event Structure establishes their different realisations as associated with a single lexical item and thus with a unique aspectual and categorial status.

In the section below, I will assess as well the categorial status of Class two property items from the perspective of the aspectual analysis that I have posited for them.

6.2.2 Class 2 property items as (Stative) adjectives

Class 2 property items are sub-divided into three classes reflecting items that are incompatible with Non-stative expression (Class 2a), those that allow for a (Non-stative) Change of state interpretation (Class 2b) and those that allow for a (Non-stative) Process interpretation (Class 2c). The examples below (recalled from Chapter 5) reflect this:

(3) (Class 2a – example (11) recalled from Chapter 5)

    a. Di siment **haad**.
       art cement hard
       'The cement is hard.'
       * 'The cement has hardened.'

    b. * Di siment a **haad**.
       art cement ASP hard
       'The cement is hardening.'

    c. * Dem **haad** di siment.
       3PL hard the cement
       'They made the cement hard.'

(4) (Example (16) recalled from Chapter 5)

    a. Di shuuz **blak**.
       ART shoes black
       'The shoe is black.'

    b. ?? Di shuuz a **blak/red**.
       ART shoes ASP black
       'The shoe is getting black.'

    c. ?? Dem **blak/red** di shuuz.
       3PL black/red ART shoes
       They are making the shoe black/blackening the shoe.'

(5) (Class 2b – example (18) recalled from Chapter 5)

    a. Di mango dem **red**.
       ART mango PL red
       'The mangoes are red.'

6.2 On the categorial status of dual aspectual forms

    b. Di mango dem **red** pan di chrii.
       ART mango PL red on ART tree
       'The mangoes got red on the tree.'

    c. Di son **red** di mango dem pan di chrii.
       ART sun red ART mango PL on ART tree
       'The sun reddened the mango.'

(6) (Class 2c – examples (20) and (21) recalled from Chapter 5)

    a. Dat de pikni **bad/ruud**!
       that LOC child bad/rude
       'That child is a bad/rude child!'

    b. Dat de pikni a **bad/ruud** lang taim.
       that LOC child ASP bad/rude long time
       'That child has been misbehaving for a long time.'

(7) a. Dem **jelas**.
       3PL jealous
       'They are jealous.'

    b. Dem a **jelas** mi fi di kyar we mi jraiv.
       3PL ASP jealous 1SG for ART car that 1SG drive
       'They are (being) jealous/envious of me because of my car.'

As shown in these examples, the items in this Class are diverse in the syntactic and semantic behaviours that they display. As shown in (3), an item such as *haad* 'hard' in JC is resistant to any Non-stative interpretation allowing neither for Imperfective aspect marking nor transitive variation. Items such as 'red' and 'black' in JC as discussed in Chapter 5, represent those items that may allow for a Non-stative Change of state interpretation. As purely colour terms, these appear as only marginally acceptable in JC as indicated in (4), but *red* is fully acceptable in idiomatic use as shown by the examples in (5). Finally, there are those items such as *bad, ruud* and *jelas* which appear in Non-stative use indicating a Process.

In spite of the variation observed in the behaviour of these items, I have argued that these all share a common Event Structure of State shown in Figure 6.3 (Figure 5.3 recalled from Chapter 5).

Based on this Event Structure, items of this type represent single eventualities that are interpreted relative to no other event. A logical implication of such an Event Structure is that items of this type will only appear in Stative (adjectival)

6 Summing up: On the categorial status of dual aspectual forms

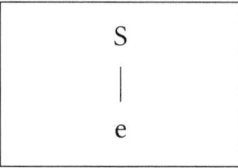

Figure 6.3: State Event Structure (Pustejovsky 1991: 56)

use. However, as we have seen, this is observationally adequate only for items displaying the behaviour of JC *haad* 'hard' which does not vary in Stativity. In the case of items with behaviour similar to that of *red* 'red' and *bad* 'bad' or *ruud* 'rude' in §5.3, I posited the introduction of elements of meaning consistent with the primitives CAUSE, BECOME and DO into their Event Structure to account for their Non-stative instantiations. Thus, while in Stative use, they reflect an Event Structure of a pure State (Figure 6.3); in Non-stative use, they reflect a derived Event Structure of Transition or Process as shown in Figure 6.4.

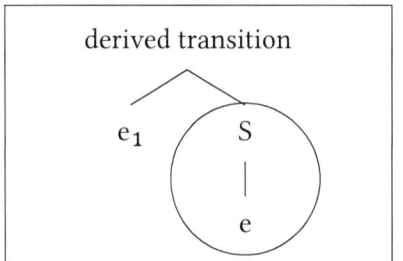 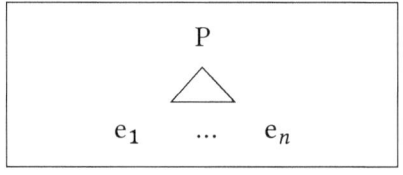

Figure 6.4: Figure 5.4 and Figure 5.5 recalled from §5.3.2. Left: An Event Structure representing derived Transition. Right: Event Structure of Process (Pustejovsky 1991: 56)

The derivation which allows for the introduction of Change in the Event Structure of similar items has been elaborated in §5.3. Consistent with the analysis that proposes derived Transition and Process Event Structure for items of this type, I posit here that this process also results in the lexical conversion of these items from (Stative) adjectives to (Non-stative) verbs. Thus, in their Non-stative instantiations, these show the behaviour of Non-stative verbs expressing either a Change of state or a Process.

The differences that may be observed between these and inherently Non-stative verbs come from the fact that items of this type are derived verbs. Thus for example, I point out in terms of semantic behaviour that those items which are derived as Transitions only express an opposition of contradiction while those that are inherent Transitions reflect an opposition of contrariety. Similarly, items which are inherently associated with the Event Structure of Process do not also allow for Stative uses, in contrast with property items which are derived to express this Event Structure. Kouwenberg (1996) observes a similar phenomenon in relation to the categorial status of such items, noting for Berbice Dutch that "derived verbs do not have all the properties of base verbs" (p. 35).

The proposal that Class 2 property items which allow for Non-stative interpretations are associated with derived Event Structures allows for observational adequacy regarding the behaviour of such items and has implications for the analysis of their categorial status. Essentially, it accounts for the variation in the appearance and aspectual denotation of these items while allowing for them to be associated with the unique Event Structure of State. This in turn allows for the proposal that items of Class 2 are associated with an inherent adjectival status even where they may vary in their appearance as (Non-stative) verbs or (Stative) adjectives.

6.3 Contribution to scholarship

This work has attempted to bring the discussion of Aspect in CECs to the fore. As indicated in Chapter 2, this area of study has to a large extent been treated under the umbrella of TMA where the focus has been on Tense rather than Aspect. The primary focus on Aspect here is in line with the observation that Aspect may be more basic than Tense in Creole languages (see Alleyne 1980 for example). From this perspective, my findings may be used to strengthen what has been for the most part a very strong intuition among authors on the analysis of Tense marking in Creoles, as being dependent on the inherent aspect of the verb (see Winford 1993, and discussion in Chapter 2).

My treatment of property items from the perspective of their aspectual behaviour diverges from what may be seen as the standard assessment of the categorial status of these items in CECs, which classifies them in predicative use as (Stative) verbs (cf. Sebba 1986; Alleyne 1980; Winford 1993, etc.). It is also distinct from the contrasting position of Seuren (1986), who argues for a status of these items as adjectives, distinct from (Stative) verbs in their ability to express causation in their variation of Stativity (see discussion of this debate in Chapter 3, §3.2). I have shown in my discussion of the debate surrounding these items that neither of these positions is tenable. Moreover, I have argued that an "either or" analysis of property items as verbs or adjectives, as strictly Non-statives or Statives is limited and given the diversity in their syntactic and aspectual be-

6 Summing up: On the categorial status of dual aspectual forms

haviours, satisfaction of both observational and explanatory adequacy requires an analysis that lends itself to an account of the flexibility that characterizes this group of items.

As we have seen, an event structure (ES) approach such as I have employed in this work allows for observation and account of both syntactic and semantic phenomena as associated with these items. The traditional approaches, as discussed in Chapters 2 and 3 of this work, have focused on their syntactic behaviours alone for a classification of their categorial status; instead, insights into the semantic structures associated with lexical items allows for what may be seen as a bottom up analysis. Essentially what I have done is to centralize focus on the lexico-semantics of these items into the discussion, taking a basic "semantics-prior" position in order to explain their flexibility in behaviour at the syntactic level. With a sensitivity to the syntax-semantics interface, where it is understood that the syntactic and semantic domains interact and impact each other, this work was able to observe more and handle more objectively the variability observed in the behaviour of property items in CECs.

When compared to previous analyses, the one I put forward here most closely resembles that of Kouwenberg (1996) in the diversity of categorial status that she notes among property items in Berbice Dutch. In her treatment, she analyses these as two classes of items, the first being assigned dual category membership as both (Process) verbs and adjectives and the second occupying only the category of adjective. This is based on the ability of the former to allow for a processual interpretation and a restriction on the latter in this respect. However, a crucial difference between our analyses is that while she argues for the group of 'adjectivals' as adjectives with a separation between those that allow for derivation into (Non-stative) verbs and those that do not, I argue for a distinction between a group of verbs and a group of adjectives underlyingly. Both groups may be expressed as either V or A; the former due to their inherent Event Structure and the latter due to morphological derivation.

Most previous attempts at analying dual aspectual forms have been subject to limitations also in that they have done so from the perspective of an account of a handful of lexical items only (e.g., Sebba 1986; Seuren 1986), whereas there is a whole group of items – so called property items – which merit an overall account. Winford (1993) rightly addressed this entire group and provided an analysis of their behaviour from the point of view of their membership in semantic classes. However, as discussed in Chapter 3, while this allows for a separation between Stative and Non-stative items within the large group, membership in a particular semantic class does not always predict the actual behaviour of an item. Furthermore, Winford provides no clear account of those items that seem to defy a categorisation as either Stative or Non-stative due to their appearance in both these uses. He appears to be cognisant of the weakness in his dependence on semantic classes in his analysis of property items as his later works (1997; 2001) relied less on these semantic classes but continued focus on syntactic tests.

Nevertheless, his intuition that there was a semantic factor involved and relevant in a categorisation of these items was no doubt justified. As I have shown, the inclusion of overarching semantic features (linked to ES) is critical in treating these items. Where authors understandably focused on the ability of these items to appear in Non-stative use and other syntactic criteria (Chapter 3) as relevant for their categorisation, my inclusion of semantic features linked to ES, allowed more clearly, I believe, for an objective categorisation of this class of items as underlyingly consisting of both verbs and adjectives.

Firstly, there is a group of items in CECs that may be characterised as Change of state verbs based on their ability to appear in Non-stative use and the ES by which they are characterised; these I refer to as Class 1 items. Like all other property items, they also appear in Stative use. However, they are distinct from all others based on the fact that, they, in Non-stative use, encode what I have elaborated as a logical opposition of contrariety. They may appear in either verbal use (which is also Non-stative in this case) or adjectival (Stative) use dependent on the aspect of the ES that is being expressed. A similarly complex situation exists for items that I classified as Class 2, which comprises forms with the ES "State." This includes three types of forms: those that I characterise as strictly Stative in their inability to appear in Non-stative use (Class 2a), but also those that, like items in Class 1, also appear in Non-stative use expressing what I identify as a Transition (Class 2b) and also those that in similar use express a Process ES (Class 2c). The semantic difference between the notion of a logical opposition of contrariety and one of contradiction facilitates my identification of Class 2b items as State items derived to express an ES of transition in contrast items in Class 1 which are inherently transition (see discussion of this in §5.2.3).

Importantly, the semantic nuances which surround this group of items demand that careful attention be paid not just to syntactic but semantic features in an attempt at their classification. While perhaps there is necessity to conduct a more in depth investigation in this vein to facilitate a more fine-grained analysis, this study is in my estimation a step along a critical path to provide a more objective analysis of these items supported by modern theoretical models. Nevertheless, from the viewpoint of the analysis undertaken in this work, an either or analysis of property items as either verbs or adjectives or based on the simple bipartite Stative/Non-stative distinction as it has been applied in Creole Studies (see Bickerton 1975; 1981/2016) is limited and misses completely the diversity in behaviour that may characterize lexical items.

In conclusion, in this work, I have posited an explicit account of items that appear in dual aspectual use in CECs – in this way shedding new light on the Stative/Non-stative distinction and its application to Creole languages. Perhaps in some small way, this analysis serves to validate and reconcile the various viewpoints that have existed on this matter in the field. Based on my analysis, the dominant viewpoint which analyses these items as Stative verbs is untenable. In essence, the ES associated with Stative verbs is distinct from the ES that we see expressed by members of this group of items. The opposing view that restricts them to being adjectives is also untenable: It is inconsistent with the diversity in observable behaviour of these items. The ES approach has thrown new light on this question and provided a flexible analysis that may be used to generalise over the behaviours of the entire group of items.

6.4 Scope for further study

It is important, given the gap that has been noted between the study of Aspect generally and what has been undertaken in Creole studies,[1] that more work be done in the field which reflects the nature of Aspect as one that is compositional. Thus, for example, where various authors have spent significant energies on the matter of grammatical aspect (which I believe to be important), there are several other elements that are involved in the domain of Aspect which remain unexplored in Creole studies. In the case of the contribution of the verb, this has for the most part been taken for granted with a majority of authors making reference to the existence of Stative and Non-stative verbs. However, as I have pointed out in this study, a basic conceptual question in the application of this distinction remained unanswered, thus weakening the strength of those analyses utilising this basic distinction.

The contribution made to Aspect by the internal argument and other elements such as adverbials, has been noted (see Jaganauth 1987 for example), but not reflected in our studies as far as a compositional approach is concerned. Thus, a clear picture of the specific lexical items that contribute a particular semantic feature has not emerged in Creole studies. Consequently there is a huge gap in the awareness of the complexity of Aspect in the works of authors in the general field as opposed to those in the field of Creole studies. This work has only

---

[1]This general observation has been made previously by authors such as Winford (1993; 1997; 2001) and also Dahl (1993).

managed to look at one element involved in Aspect and attempted to account for the basic intuition associated with the Stative/Non-stative distinction and the problem raised by forms which appear in both Stative and Non-stative use.

It is my expectation that work can be done to address the different compositional levels of Aspect in CECs. For example, the specific contribution of the internal argument as it regards quantification and scope as well as the role of adverbials should lend insights into how Creole languages compare to other languages that have been studied in this area. Also, given the variability in the aspectual behaviour of property items within and across Creoles, there is scope for the study of their behaviour in specific Creoles. Study along these lines will give further insights into the similarities and differences among Creoles thus strengthening the impact that we may be able to have in the context of the larger theoretical field.

References

Alleyne, Mervyn C. 1980. *Comparative Afro-American*. Ann Arbor: Karoma.

Alleyne, Mervyn C. 1987. Predicate structures in Saramaccan. In Mervyn C. Alleyne (ed.), *Studies in Saramaccan language structure* (Caribbean Culture Studies 2), 71–88. Mona: University of the West Indies.

Allsopp, Richard. 1983. The Creole treatment of passive. In Lawrence D. Carrington & Ramon Todd-Dandaré (eds.), *Studies in Caribbean language*, 142–154. St. Augustine, Trinidad: Society for Caribbean Linguistics.

Andersen, R. W. 1990. Papiamentu tense-aspect, with special attention to discourse. In John Singler (ed.), *Pidgin and Creole tense-mood-aspect systems*, 59–96. Amsterdam: John Benjamins.

Bailey, Beryl Loftman. 1966. *Jamaican Creole syntax: A transformational approach*. Cambridge: Cambridge University Press.

Bennett, Michael & Barbara H. Partee. 2004. Toward the logic of tense and aspect in English. In Susan Rothstein (ed.), *Structuring events: A study in the semantics of aspect* (Explorations in Semantics), 59–107. Oxford: Blackwell.

Bickerton, Derek. 1981/2016. *Roots of language*. Berlin: Language Science Press. DOI:10.17169/langsci.b91.109

Bickerton, Derek. 1975. *Dynamics of a Creole system*. Cambridge: Cambridge University Press.

Borer, Hagit. 2005. *Structuring sense: In name only*. Vol. 1. Oxford: Oxford University Press.

Carter, Richard J. 1988. Some linking regularities: Papers by Richard Carter. In Richard J. Carter, Beth Levin & Carol L. Tenny (eds.), *On linking* (Lexicon Project Working Papers 25), 1–92. Cambridge, MA: Center for Cognitive Science, Massachusetts Institute of Technology.

Chierchia, Gennaro & Sally McConnell-Ginet. 1992. *Meaning and grammar: An introduction to semantics*. 1st edn. Cambridge, MA: The MIT Press.

Chomsky, Noam. 1965. *Aspects of the theory of syntax*. Cambridge, MA: The MIT Press.

Comrie, Bernard. 1976. *Aspect: An introduction to the study of verbal aspect and related problems*. Cambridge: Cambridge University Press.

References

Dahl, Östen. 1981. On the definition of the telic-atelic (bounded/non-bounded) distinction. In Philip Tedeschi & Annie Zaenen (eds.), *Tense and aspect*, 79–90. New York: Academic Press.

Dahl, Östen. 1985. *Tense and aspect systems*. Oxford: Blackwell.

Dahl, Östen. 1993. Review of Pidgin and Creole tense-mood-aspect systems. *Studies in Language* 17. 251–258.

Dixon, R.M.W. 1977. Where have all the adjectives gone? *Studies in Language* 1. 19–80. DOI:10.1075/sl.1.1.04dix

Dowty, David R. 1979. *Word meaning and Montague grammar: The semantics of verbs and times in generative semantics and in Montague's PTQ* (Studies in Linguistics and Philosophy 7). Berlin: Springer. DOI:10.1007/978-94-009-9473-7

Dowty, David R. 2006. *Compositionality as an empirical problem*. Columbus, OH: Department of Linguistics, Ohio State University.

Filip, H. 2000. The quantization puzzle: The converging perspectives of lexical semantics and syntax. In Carol L. Tenny & James Pustejovsky (eds.), *Events as grammatical objects*, 39–93. Stanford: CSLI.

Garey, Howard B. 1957. Verbal aspect in French. *Language* 33(2). 91–110.

Gooden, Shelome. 2008. Discourse aspects of tense marking in Belizean Creole. *English World-Wide* 29(3). 306–346. DOI:10.1075/eww.29.3.04goo

Grimshaw, Jane. 1990. *Argument structure*. Cambridge, MA: The MIT Press.

Guéron, Jacqueline. 2008. On the difference between telicity and perfectivity. *Lingua* 118(11). 1816–1840. DOI:10.1016/j.lingua.2007.04.005

Holm, John A. 1988. *Pidgins and Creoles: Theory and structure*. Vol. 1. Cambridge: Cambridge University Press.

Horn, Laurence R. 1989. *A natural history of negation*. Chicago, IL: University of Chicago Press.

Jackendoff, Ray. 1972. *Semantic interpretation in generative grammar*. Cambridge, MA: The MIT Press.

Jackendoff, Ray. 1975. Morphological and semantic regularities in the lexicon. *Language* 51(3). 639–671.

Jackendoff, Ray. 1990. *Semantic structures*. Cambridge, MA: The MIT Press.

Jackendoff, Ray. 1996. The proper treatment of measuring out, telicity and perhaps even quantification in English. *Natural Language & Linguistic Theory* 14(2). 305–354.

Jaganauth, Dhanaiswary. 1987. *Predicate structures in Guyanese Creole*. Mona: The University of the West Indies MA thesis.

Klein, Wolfgang. 1994. *Time in language*. London: Routledge.

Kouwenberg, Silvia. 1996. The relation between adjectives and verbs, with special reference to Berbice Dutch Creole: Papers in honour of Professor Mervyn Alleyne on the occasion of his sixtieth birthday. In Pauline Christie (ed.), *Caribbean language issues old and new*, 27–40. Barbados/Jamaica/Trinidad & Tobago: The Press University of the West Indies.

Kouwenberg, Silvia & Claire Lefebvre. 2007. A new analysis of the Papiamentu clause structure. *Probus: International Journal of Latin and Romance Linguistics* 19. 37–73. DOI:10.1515/PROBUS.2007.002

Krifka, Manfred. 1998. The origins of telicity. In Susan Rothstein (ed.), *Events and grammar*, 197–235. Dordrecht: Kluwer.

Krifka, Manfred. 2001. The mereological approach to aspectual composition. Paper presented at Conference perspectives on Aspect. University of Utrecht, OTS Dec. 12–14, 2001.

Larson, Richard K. 1988. On the double object construction. *Linguistic Inquiry* 19(3). 335–391.

Levin, Beth. 1993. *English verb classes and alternations: A preliminary investigation*. Chicago, IL: Chicago University Press.

Lyons, John. 1977. *Semantics*. Vol. 2. Cambridge: Cambridge University Press.

MacDonald, Jonathan E. 2008. *The syntactic nature of inner aspect: A minimalist perspective*. Amsterdam: John Benjamins Publishing.

McCawley, James D. 1968. Lexical insertion in a transformational grammar without deep structure. *Proceedings of the Chicago Linguistic Society (CLS)* 4. 71–80.

McCawley, James D. 1973. Prelexical syntax: Papers on syntactic and semantic topics. In James D. McCawley (ed.), *Grammar and meaning*, 343–356. Tokyo: Taishukan Publishing Company.

Migge, Bettina. 2000. The origin of the syntax and semantics of property items in the Surinamese Plantation Creole. In John McWhorter (ed.), *Language change and language contact in Pidgins and Creoles*, 201–233. Amsterdam: John Benjamins Publishing.

Moens, Marc & Mark Steedman. 1988. Temporal ontology and temporal reference. *Computational Linguistics* 14(2). 15–28.

Mourelatos, Alexander P. D. 1981. Events, processes, and states. *Syntax and Semantics* 14. 191–211.

Mufwene, Salikoko. 1984. *Stativity and the progressive*. Bloomington: Indiana University Linguistics Club.

References

Pustejovsky, James. 1988. The geometry of events. In Carol L. Tenny (ed.), *Studies in generative approaches to aspect lexicon* (Project Working Papers 24). Cambridge, MA: Center for Cognitive Science at MIT.

Pustejovsky, James. 1991. The syntax of event structure. *Cognition* 41(1-3). 47–81. DOI:10.1016/0010-0277(91)90032-Y

Ramchand, Gillian Catriona. 2008. Perfectivity as aspectual definiteness: Time and the event in Russian. *Lingua* 118. 1690–1715. DOI:10.1016/j.lingua.2007.03.008

Rothstein, Susan. 2004. *Structuring events: A study in the semantics of lexical aspect*. Oxford: Blackwell.

Sebba, Mark. 1986. Adjectives and copulas in Sranan Tongo. *Journal of Pidgin and Creole Languages* 1(1). 109–121.

Seuren, Pieter A. M. 1986. Adjectives as adjectives in Sranan: A reply to Sebba. *Journal of Pidgin and Creole Languages* 1(1). 123–134.

Sidnell, Jack. 2002. Habitual and imperfective in Guyanese Creole. *Journal of Pidgin and Creole Languages* 17(2). 151–189.

Smith, Carlota S. 1983. A theory of aspectual choice. *Language* 59. 479–501.

Smith, Carlota S. 1991. *The parameter of aspect*. Dordrecht: Kluwer.

Solomon, Denis. 1993. *The speech of Trinidad: A reference grammar*. Trinidad: University of the West Indies.

Tenny, Carol L. 1994. *Aspectual roles and the syntax-semantics interface*. Dordrecht: Kluwer Academic Publishers.

Tenny, Carol L. & James Pustejovsky. 2000. A history of events in linguistic theory. In Carol L. Tenny & James Pustejovsky (eds.), *Events as grammatical objects the converging perspectives of lexical semantics and syntax*, 3–32. Stanford: CSLI.

Travis, Lisa. 1991. Inner aspect and the structure of VP. *North East Linguistic Society (NELS)* 22.

Travis, Lisa. 2000. Event structure in syntax: Events as grammatical objects the converging perspectives of lexical semantics and syntax. In Carol L. Tenny & James Pustejovsky (eds.), *A history of events in linguistic theory*, 145–185. Stanford: CSLI.

Travis, Lisa. 2010. *Inner aspect: The articulation of VP* (Studies in Natural Language and Linguistic Theory 80). Berlin/Heidelberg: Springer Science & Business Media.

Vendler, Zeno. 1957. Verbs and times. *The Philosophical Review* 66(2). 143–160. DOI:10.2307/2182371

Vendler, Zeno. 1967. Verbs and times. In *Linguistics in Philosophy*. Ithaca, NY: Cornell University Press. Revised version of Vendler, Zeno. 1957. Verbs and times, *Philosophical Review* 66: 143-60.

Verkuyl, Henk J. 1972. *On the compositional nature of the aspects*. Dordrecht: Reidel.

Verkuyl, Henk J. 1996. *A theory of aspectuality: The interaction between temporal and atemporal structure*. Cambridge: Cambridge University Press.

Verkuyl, Henk J. 1999. *Aspectual issues: Studies in time and quantity*. Stanford, CA: CSLI.

Voorhoeve, Jan. 1957. The verbal system of Sranan. *Lingua* 6. 374–396.

Winford, Donald. 1993. *Predication in Caribbean English Creoles*. Amsterdam: John Benjamins Publishing.

Winford, Donald. 1997. Property items and predication in Sranan. *Journal of Pidgin and Creole Languages* 12(2). 237–301.

Winford, Donald. 2000. Tense and and aspect in Sranan and the Creole prototype. In John McWhorter (ed.), *Language change and language contact in pidgins and Creoles*, 383–442. Amsterdam: John Benjamins.

Winford, Donald. 2001. On the typology of Creole TMA systems: Evidence from Caribbean Creoles. In *Society for Caribbean linguistics 2000*, 320–328. Mona: University of the West Indies.

Youssef, Valerie. 1995. Tense–aspect in Tobagonian English: A dynamic transitional system. *English World-Wide* 16(2). 195–213.

Youssef, Valerie. 2003. How perfect is perfective marking?: An analysis of the terminological problems in the description of some tense-aspect categories in Creoles. *Journal of Pidgin and Creole Languages* 18. 81–105.

Name index

Alleyne, Mervyn C., 9, 19, 24–26, 28, 29, 48, 52–54, 58, 127, 143
Allsopp, Richard, 102
Andersen, R. W, 43, 69

Bailey, Beryl Loftman, 129
Bennett, Michael, 8
Bickerton, Derek, 10, 12, 13, 15, 19, 20, 27, 28, 30, 31, 33–35, 40, 41, 43, 45, 51, 54, 55, 69, 107, 109, 120, 133, 145, 146
Borer, Hagit, 8

Carter, Richard J., 16, 86, 87, 90, 99, 107, 127, 131
Chierchia, Gennaro, 96
Chomsky, Noam, 101
Comrie, Bernard, 1, 2, 5, 12–14, 16, 22, 23, 26, 85, 87, 107

Dahl, Östen, 5, 6, 33, 146
Dixon, R.M.W., 10, 12, 58, 70, 71, 108
Dowty, David R., 4, 6, 14, 16, 49, 86, 87, 90, 99, 100, 107, 131

Filip, H, 5

Garey, Howard B., 5, 7
Gooden, Shelome, 19, 20, 34, 48, 50, 55, 69, 107, 109, 120, 133
Grimshaw, Jane, 86, 90, 91, 107, 114, 128, 129, 131
Guéron, Jacqueline, 2, 3, 111

Holm, John A., 51
Horn, Laurence R., 115

Jackendoff, Ray, 1, 5, 7, 85, 90, 92, 94, 95, 100, 101
Jaganauth, Dhanaiswary, 9, 12, 15, 19, 20, 30, 34, 37, 40, 41, 45, 55, 58, 68, 70, 106, 107, 109, 120, 146

Klein, Wolfgang, 1, 14
Kouwenberg, Silvia, 9, 13, 15, 19, 43, 57, 58, 65–67, 82, 136–139, 143, 144
Krifka, Manfred, 1, 5, 7, 8, 85, 95

Larson, Richard K., 131
Lefebvre, Claire, 43
Levin, Beth, 10, 47, 70, 86, 90, 97, 101–104, 107
Lyons, John, 3, 8, 109–111

MacDonald, Jonathan E., 1, 6, 7, 10, 86, 106
McCawley, James D., 16, 86, 87, 90, 97, 99, 107, 131
McConnell-Ginet, Sally, 96
Migge, Bettina, 9, 67, 68
Moens, Marc, 5
Mourelatos, Alexander P. D., 1, 5, 85
Mufwene, Salikoko, 50

Partee, Barbara H., 8

Pustejovsky, James, 1, 4, 6, 10, 16, 36, 39, 70, 86, 89–95, 107, 109, 112–114, 120, 123, 127, 129, 131, 134, 138, 139, 142

Ramchand, Gillian Catriona, 1
Rothstein, Susan, 1, 5, 12, 86

Sebba, Mark, 9, 15, 19, 57–61, 65, 67, 82, 137, 143, 144
Seuren, Pieter A. M., 9, 15, 19, 57, 61–63, 65, 82, 137, 143, 144
Sidnell, Jack, 19, 20, 26, 30, 45–47, 49, 54, 55, 70, 107
Smith, Carlota S., 1, 2, 4, 5, 14, 109, 110, 121
Solomon, Denis, 51, 52
Steedman, Mark, 5

Tenny, Carol L., 1, 5–8, 12, 85, 86, 94, 95, 106
Travis, Lisa, 1, 2, 98, 131

Vendler, Zeno, 4, 6, 26, 30, 85, 86, 89, 109, 111
Verkuyl, Henk J., 1, 5–8, 12, 14, 20, 85, 86, 88, 95, 106, 109
Voorhoeve, Jan, 9, 15, 19, 20, 22, 24, 27–30, 52, 54, 58

Winford, Donald, 9, 10, 12, 15, 19, 20, 34, 40–43, 49, 51–53, 57, 58, 64, 66–72, 74, 82, 107, 108, 120, 129, 133, 137, 143, 144, 146

Youssef, Valerie, 27, 51, 52

Language index

Belizean Creole, 42, 50
Berbice Dutch Creole, 65–67, 143, 144

Conservative Guyanese Creole, 45, 47

Finnish, 2

Gullah, 24, 25
Guyanese Creole, 15, 24, 25, 28, 29, 31, 34, 35, 37, 42, 45, 45^{21}, 66^{6}, 68

Jamaican Creole, 6, 6^{4}, 7, 11, 12, 14–16, 24–26, 38, 42, 58, 66^{6}, 73–76, 76^{11}, 77–82, 86, 91, 96, 100, 102^{6}, 108, 109, 109^{2}, 112–116, 118, 119^{3}, 120, 123–130, 134, 136, 138, 139, 141, 142

Krio, 24

Papiamentu, 43

Saramaccan, 24, 65, 138
Sranan, 20, 21, 23–26, 42, 43, 58, 59, 61–63, 64^{3}, 65, 66, 76^{11}, 123, 127

Subject index

Accomplishment, 6, 10^8, 13, 49, 86, 89
Achievement, 6, 10^8, 13, 49, 86
Activity, 6, 10^8, 13, 49, 86, 89, 91, 99, 100, 115, 130
adjectival use, 17, 136, 138
Adjective, 61
Agent, 17, 38, 89, 96, 98, 99, 102–104, 112, 123, 124, 128, 131
Aspect, v, 1, 1^1, 2, 4–6, 8, 10, 10^8, 12–15, 19, 20, 20^3, 24, 27, 30, 34, 39, 42, 43, 43^{19}, 45, 46, 48, 48^{24}, 49–52, 54, 60, 68–71, 85–87, 88^2, 91, 107, 111, 133, 134, 143, 146, 147
aspect marker, 29, 30, 34, 35, 37, 43, 43^{20}, 44, 45, 96, 137
aspectual flexibility, 14, 42
aspectual marking, 29, 30
aspectual outlook, 1, 29, 39, 42, 43
aspectual status, 9^5, 10, 11, 15, 19, 21, 28, 39, 57, 58, 68, 71, 71^8, 82, 83, 135, 136
Atelic, 5, 7, 8, 13, 89, 105
attributive position, 65, 66^6

body-part possessor ascension alternation, 101, 103

categorial status, 9, 9^5, 10, 12, 15, 17, 19, 21, 57, 58, 63, 65, 67, 68, 82, 83, 132, 133, 135–137, 139, 143, 144

Causative, 98, 99, 112
causative variation, 63, 64
causative verb, 32
change of state interpretation, 11
Completive, 52, 53
complex morphological verb, 78
compositional approach, 14, 146
conative alternation, 101, 104

dual aspectual behaviour, 87, 105, 108
dual aspectual forms, 12, 15, 20, 47, 55, 58, 64, 71^8, 82, 86, 87, 90, 92, 96, 100, 106, 107, 112, 119, 121, 131–134, 144
dual aspectual use, 108, 111, 146

event structure, 91, 144
event type, 16, 91, 94, 114, 119, 120, 123, 137, 139
external argument, 98, 99

grammatical aspect, 1, 1^1, 13, 15, 19, 21, 24, 27, 29, 30, 42–45, 48, 51–53, 89, 146

Habitual, 23, 24, 25^6, 30, 37^{15}, 45, 46, 46^{22}, 53, 54, 89
habitual meaning, 46

Imperfective, 1, 2, 14, 21, 23, 26, 26^8, 27, 29, 30, 34, 35, 37, 37^{15}, 43, 43^{20}, 44, 45, 52, 54, 66, 67,

Subject index

73, 74^9, 76, 78, 81, 109, 111–113, 137, 141
Inchoative, 21, 112
inchoative variation, 103
inherent aspect, 3, 12–14, 16, 19, 20, 26^8, 34, 39, 43–45, 48, 49, 86, 106, 109, 111, 143
inherent aspectual status, 117
inherent event, 113
inner aspect, 1, 5, 10^8, 13, 14, 20^2
internal argument, 5–8, 13, 16^{12}, 88–90, 94, 98, 102, 103, 105, 106, 106^7, 146, 147

lexical aspect, 20^2, 49, 51
lexical level, 12, 16, 42, 49
lexical specification, 32, 47, 55, 70, 70^7
lexico-semantic domain, 48, 49
logical opposition of contradiction, 114–116
logical opposition of contrariety, 114, 116, 118, 136, 137, 145

middle alternation, 102
morphological operation, 100
morphological process, 11, 100, 127

null marker, 27, 51, 52

observational adequacy, 30, 74, 79, 134, 143
outer aspect, 1, 13

Past, 27, 29, 34, 34^{13}, 40, 41, 51, 52, 89, 133
Perfect, 52, 53
Perfective, 1, 2, 14, 24–27, 29, 42, 43, 52, 53, 67

perfective aspect, 2, 11, 23, 25, 26, 28^{10}, 36, 44, 54
perfective meaning, 25
predicate adjective, 59
predicative use, 58–60, 143
Process, v, 10, 11, 16, 17, 33, 45, 80, 82, 83, 90, 91, 93–96, 100, 106, 108–111, 113, 114, 116, 118–121, 124, 128, 129, 131, 134, 137, 138, 140–145
Progressive, 2–4, 12, 21, 23, 24, 26^8, 30, 30^{11}, 33, 37^{15}, 42, 43, 45, 46, 54, 71, 71^8, 73, 96, 108–113, 115, 118, 119^3, 121, 124, 129, 130, 133
progressive criterion, 4, 109, 110, 112
property item, 124, 136

Resultative, 52

semantic behaviour, 11, 114–116, 137, 142
semantic category, 73, 81
semi-copula, 76^{10}, 78
single eventuality, 10, 113
State, 6, 9–11, 13, 16, 17, 36, 37^{15}, 38, 49, 64, 79, 80, 86–88, 90–92, 92^4, 93–96, 99, 106, 108, 110–116, 118–121, 123, 124, 127–129, 131, 134, 137, 138, 141–143, 145
Change of, 3, 4, 9, 11, 16, 23, 32, 36, 36^{14}, 45, 71, 71^8, 73, 74, 78, 80–82, 90, 93, 97, 99, 100, 102, 103, 106, 108, 109, 109^2, 111, 112, 114–116, 118, 119, 121, 123, 126, 127, 131, 134–137, 139–142, 145

Stative, 1, 3, 4, 8, 9^6, 10, 10^7, 11–13, 15–17, 19, 20, 20^2, 26, 26^8, 28–30, 30^{11}, 31–38, 38^{16}, 39–51, 55, 57, 57^1, 57^2, 58–60, 63, 64, 64^3, 67–71, 73, 74, 76, 76^{11}, 78, 81–83, 85, 88–90, 95–97, 101, 105–111, 114, 117–121, 123, 125, 126, 128, 129, 131–136, 138, 139, 141–147

Stative/Non-stative distinction, 85–106

Stativity, 2, 4, 12, 19–21, 23, 32, 33, 39, 47, 49–51, 54, 55, 57^2, 64, 67, 68, 70, 71, 71^8, 73, 74, 76, 81, 85, 106, 108–110, 119^3, 120, 137, 142, 143

stem form, 28

syntax-semantics interface, 5, 97, 144

Telic, 5, 7, 8, 13, 49, 89, 105

Telicity, 7, 8, 48, 85, 95, 106, 106^7

Tense, v, 10^7, 15, 20, 24, 26–31, 33, 34, 41–43, 46, 48, 48^{24}, 51, 69, 89, 107, 133, 143

Transition, 10, 11, 16, 17, 36, 39, 90, 91, 92^4, 93–95, 97, 106, 109, 111, 113, 115–117, 119–121, 124–127, 131, 132, 134, 137–139, 142, 145

Transitive, 112

transitive alternation, 121

transitive variation, 11, 74^9, 113, 117, 141

transitory states, 71

unmarked verb, 21, 22, 27–30, 48, 133

unprefixed form, 21, 23

verbal use, 17, 136, 145

viewpoint aspect, 1–4, 14, 43, 121